CW00486571

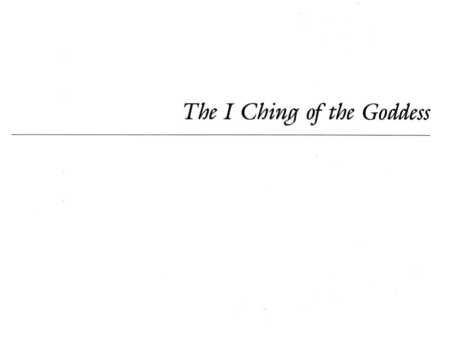

The I Ching of the Goddess

Also by Barbara G. Walker:

The Woman's Encyclopedia of Myths and Secrets
The Secrets of the Tarot: Origins, History, and Symbolism
The Crone: Woman of Age, Wisdom, and Power
The Barbara Walker Tarot Deck

Barbara G. Walker

The I Ching
of the Goddess

PERENNIAL LIBRARY

HARPER & ROW, SAN FRANCISCO

Cambridge, Hagerstown, New York, Philadelphia, Washington
London, Mexico City, São Paulo, Singapore, Sydney

THE I CHING OF THE GODDESS.
Copyright © 1986 by Barbara G. Walker.
All rights reserved. Printed in the United States of
America. No part of this book may be used or
reproduced in any manner whatsoever without
written permission except in the case of brief quo-
tations embodied in critical articles and reviews.
For information address Harper & Row, Publish-
ers, Inc., 10 East 53rd Street, New York, NY 10022.
Published simultaneously in Canada by Fitzhenry
& Whiteside, Limited, Toronto.

Designed by Leigh McLellan

Library of Congress Cataloging-in-Publication Data

Walker, Barbara G.
  The I Ching of the goddess.

  Bibliography: p.
  1. Divination.   2. I ching.   3. Goddesses.
  4. Feminism—Religious aspects.   I. Title.
BF1751.W35 1986   133.3'3   86-45029
ISBN 0-06-250924-1

        89 90 HC 5 4

To Alan, who saw the system

Contents

1

The Family
of the Elements

Once upon a time, six or seven thousand years ago, there was a universal creation myth with versions known in every part of the then civilized world. Vestiges of this universal myth still appear in the traditions of Egypt, Greece, Persia, India, the Middle East, China, and Japan. Though the myth was matriarchal in its proposition that all the elements of creation arose from the womb of a cosmic Mother, traces of it also appear even in the patriarchal Judeo-Christian Bible. By putting together the common features of various versions of this creation myth, we can reconstruct some of the thought patterns of our earliest ancestors, which gave rise to many revered systems of representation and comprehension, such as sacred alphabets, hieroglyphics, mathematics, calendars, divinatory procedures, and theories of symbolism. Prominent among such ancient systems is the Chinese I Ching.

According to the universal creation myth, the world began in the womb of the Great Mother during her formless phase, before she differentiated anything from anything else. In this phase she assumed no shape or physical boundary even for herself. She took on the aspect of a vast, dark, semiliquid mass of potential energy and matter intermixed. Envisioned in India as Kali-Maya, the Formless Mother, she had the related names of Tiamat in Babylon, Temu in Egypt, Themis in pre-Hellenic Greece, and Tehom in Syria and Canaan. The latter was the word that later biblical writers used for the female "Deep" of Genesis.

Among the Hebrews she was also called *tohu bohu*, Primal Chaos, because the elements were so inextricably mingled in her that wet could not be distinguished from dry, nor hot from cold. Everything was homogeneously mixed and unformed. Yet the darkness of Chaos possessed the power that would result in the act of creation and cosmic birthgiving, when the elements would separate, appear, and begin to combine in their many ways to produce all the phenomena of the living world.

Since the oldest images of creation were derived from the basic idea of birth, which primitives perceived as the only possible origin of things, this precondition of Primal Chaos was drawn directly from the archaic theory that the blood-filled womb could magically create its offspring by somehow clotting or curdling its own semiliquid substance into a new, living body. Thus we often find the primordial Mother described by such titles as Ocean of Blood, Red Sea, Nether Upsurge, or Fountain of the Deep. Babylonians attributed to her a massive menstrual flow lasting three years and three months, a "fountain" that contained enough powerful creative mana to vitalize all future beings until the end of the present world.

Early mythographers knew nothing of fatherhood. They believed the process of conception was started by some mysterious movement, dance, or heart rhythm of the mother herself, which could churn the womb's divine blood as women churned milk into butter, causing it to solidify and produce its "fruit." This was one reason why primitive women's dances were full of pelvis and belly movements, dating back to the long ages when they believed such movements could magically bring about their own motherhood.

Even when some notion of fatherhood began to filter through ancient societies, it was inadequately explained by all sorts of odd theories. Some said the necessary churning movement was provided by sexual intercourse, but the true seed of creation lay only in a woman's body. Some said the male role was to help "feed" an embryo before birth. Still, mothers remained the only "blood" relatives because only mothers were thought to make their children out of their own blood.

Many traditions speak of the mother-heart principle, holding the whole power of creation. Two manifestations of the same thing in archaic belief were the dance of the primal Goddess over her own infinite sea of blood and the famous Dance of the Heart within the body. Both represented the female power to make and maintain life.

At the beginning of all things, The Goddess's mother-heart generated a tremendous energy that could clot the churning Chaos, separate and define its component elements, and bring about the cosmic organization that the Greeks called Diakosmos (the Goddess's Ordering), to carry out her plan for a new cycle of existence. From this cosmic order arose all human systems—physical, mathematical, graphic, or rhythmic.

Egyptians called this mother-heart principle the *ab*: in hieroglyphics, a dancing figure. Significantly, the Hebrews took the same word to mean "father." However, the basic idea of familylike unity and continuity of life in the universe was not a patriarchal idea. Under father gods, the world was a hierarchical pecking order rather than a network of relationship. When it was believed that all life was created from the same Mother-blood, every form was seen as related to every other form by the most vital bond of all. People felt closer to each other and to the world around them, where all things seemed animate. Even animals slain for food were brethren who must be treated with respect and prayerfully thanked for the "voluntary" sacrifice of their flesh for the lives of others.

The Egyptian concept of the *ab* included not only the soul given each individual by his/her own mother's heart but also the hidden heart of the universe, which by its rhythms controlled every cycle of seasons, lives, fates, births, and deaths. This was the spirit of "transformations" mentioned in the Book of the Dead, or of "changes" as the Oriental sages said. The Chinese I Ching means "Book of Changes." In ancient Eastern thought, existence was never static but always a becoming. Each life and all lives were in the process of eternal change, as the karmic wheel turned through all its recurrent cycles.

If we search the oldest traditions for a beginning of beginnings—the earliest roots of the creation myth—we find tantalizing hints of a once coherent story that has been revised over and over, has been garbled, slanted, and reversed in gender by countless male scholars seeking to transfer to their own gods the originally feminine First Cause. One such hint connected with the I Ching is the Chinese name for the primordial formless Mother, Nu-Kua: a name also found in variant spellings in Hindu, Egyptian, Mesopotamian, and Greek creation stories. Chinese traditions date tales about Nu-Kua back to at least 2500 B.C. Her image is still revered today in the northern provinces. Another version of her, Kuan-Yin or "The Woman," is a universal Goddess of marriage and of women generally. The original corpus of the I Ching is called Pa Kua (Eight Trigrams), and the sixty-four hexagrams are all known as *kua*, a linguistic derivative from Nu-Kua the Primal Mother.

India had a creation myth about Ma Nu or "Mother Nu," whose central feature was a primal ocean covering and containing all things at the beginning of time. The patriarchal Vedic tradition masculinized Ma Nu into a flood hero sailing on the primal ocean, perhaps drawn from earlier images of the Goddess's creative dance on the surface of her Deep. The male Ma Nu became a prototype for other flood heroes like Sumerian Ziusudra, Babylonian Ut-Napishtim, and Hebrew Noah (Nu); but "his" name still meant Mother Nu.

Sumerians also called this primal creatress Na-Mu or Mamu. Pre-Hellenic Greeks called her No-Me or Eurynome, Universal Ruler. Ancient Egyptians personified Ma Nu as the cosmic water-womb preceding creation and also as the swallowing aspect of the Goddess who daily took back into her dark abyss the same sun god she bore in the beginning, so he could arise each morning, born again and hailed by his worshipers with the ritual phrase "He is risen."

Egyptian scriptures gave the characteristics of the primordial womb spirit as Darkness, Eternity, Fluid, and Night—in various dialects, Nu, Nun, Naunet, Nut, Nuit, or Neith. Such characteristics recall unconscious memories of intrauterine life, perhaps accessible to introspective adult mystics searching internally for their own beginning. As the Mother who existed prior to all beginnings, Ma Nu organized out of her chaos-womb the four basic elements from which all subsequent matter would be formed. Each one of the four was personified in Egyptian tradition by a male-female pair of Great Deities. These sibling-consorts and their Mother-creatress became the original family of elementals known as the Ennead or "Nine Great Ones." This concept pertains to the study of the I Ching, which also arranged the same elements in a family of male-female pairs.

Perhaps the one most truly universal idea, found in every ancient civilization and even in our own modern society, is the erroneous idea that there are only four elements: water, fire, earth, and air. Even among educated people there are some who still think the elemental quality of these four disparate things is obvious. This notion has been so ever-present in all bodies of conventional wisdom that hardly anyone remembers when and where it was first heard.

Throughout European history as well as other histories, this strange idea was consistently taken for granted. It is still given credence, even in a scientific age that has identified more than a hundred real elements, none of them the classical four. The ancients were not scientific enough to recognize any of the real elements for what they are, not even the familiar metallic ones (copper, iron, gold, silver, tin, and so on). But why did they think it obvious that water, fire, earth, and air had to be the building blocks of everything in the world?

Here is the answer.

Apart from cannibalism—which fell into disrepute except as applied to the holy communion of gods' bodies—these four pseudoelements represented the only four possible ways of disposing of the dead, which returned them to an "elemental" condition. Water stood for boat burial, fire for cremation, earth for interment, and air for exposure to the carrion-eating creatures of the atmosphere.

The worldwide tendency to worship dead ancestors, which many anthropologists see as the original impulse toward god making, set up the four elemental spirits to embody those ancestors whose souls had gone into them. There was no such hard-and-fast distinction between the individual and the environment as is recognized today. Those who had died were thought to have literally become part of the living water, living fire, living earth, sky, cloud, or wind. Such ghosts and disembodied souls were everywhere. Thus ancestor worship fostered reverence for the environment.

People who cremated their dead tended to worship fire and personify fire gods. People who sent the dead out to sea, like the Vikings, worshiped the abyssal water womb as the divine Mother who would give them rebirth. Agricultural people tended to plant their dead in the earth and to personify the Earth Mother as holy ancestress of humanity, trusting her to resurrect her children from her terrestrial body as she similarly resurrected the seed. Nomadic people tended to expose their dead to the open sky, believing the vultures would carry them to the ancestral heaven, where they would become airy ghosts or perhaps receive astral ("starry") bodies and join the hosts of the stars under Mother Moon.

Such principles coexisted and interpenetrated for thousands of years. Most people forgot their original rationale but remembered the titles of their "elements," personified the elemental deities, and devised ever more ingenious pseudoreasons for their own funerary customs. However, the source of the four elements in funerary practice and ancestor worship seems incontrovertible. To this day, American Indians worship dead ancestors as having become part of the environment, in the same sense as postmortem absorption into the elements was a basic tenet of ancient faiths.

To prehistoric Chinese as to prehistoric Egyptians, the elements arising from the womb of Nu formed a family of couples, who usually entered later mythology as incestuous brother-sister consorts. Sometimes, early Oriental traditions envisioned this first-created eightfold family as a father and mother called Air (or Heaven) and Earth, with Fire and Water as their male and female children, and two other offspring of each sex to make up the magic eight.

Apparently, it was necessary to duplicate each elemental spirit to the total of eight because 8 was the first cubed number, regarded with awe as the expression of all dimensions in space. Also, the ancients generally set some kind of intermediary between the pure essence of divinity and the weak, finite senses of mortals. Just as human eyes couldn't behold the sun's essential fire without being blinded but could look steadily at a flame, so it was thought each divine element must be brought down to the level of human comprehension by assuming an earthly form or a humanlike manifestation—the basic Son-of-God or Logos theory, which was common everywhere in the ancient world.

Therefore, each elemental spirit was often paired with another spirit, representative of the same element as it commonly affects human beings or is perceived by them. For example, the I Ching system includes both a transcendent Air essence, identified with the impalpable Heavenly Father or World Oversoul, and another less remote essence called Breath, or

Wind, meaning the air as its motion can be felt by human senses, and as it moves in and out of the body to animate all air-breathing creatures with small portions of the heavenly power.

Similarly, there is an essential Water and also another kind of water called Sea, Lake, Marsh, and such manifestations of Water in daily experience. There is an essential Earth and also another kind of earth towering up before human eyes as a clearly perceptible Mountain. There is an essential Fire and also another kind of fire coming down to earth from the sphere of the sun, as lightning (probably the original source of the hearth fire), whose voice speaks through the medium of the I Ching in the form of Thunder.

Like the Egyptian Ennead, these eight elements and semielements formed the basis of I Ching divinations: Air, Breath, Water, Sea, Earth, Mountain, Fire, Thunder. Like many other systems of divination, the I Ching was founded on the theory that random mixing of the system's units would imitate the constant mixing of elements in the cosmos, to bring the incomprehensible future and the secret plans of the gods into human understanding. The same idea underlies cartomancy or divination by Tarot cards, whose four suits also represented the same four elements mixed together in various proportions by shuffling the deck.

One important difference between the I Ching and the Tarot is that the latter was adaptable to many different kinds of layouts, with fluid, open-ended interpretations subject to the insight or creative imagination of the reader. The Chinese preferred a more formal, cut-and-dried system with individual variations firmly controlled and reduced to a minimum. Unlike the Tarot, then, the I Ching is not just a divinatory tool, accessible to the illiterate and the literate alike, but a book of written, established, traditional interpretations for every possible combination of the eight units. The total number of possible interpretations then reaches the square of 8, or sixty-four possible combinations.

The Chinese devised a simple symbolism of trigrams—three straight lines—to represent the elemental units of their system. According to what they perceived as a natural duality in the alternation of cyclic forces (summer/winter, male/female, dark/light, birth/death, and so on), they combined the principles of Yang and Yin as solid and broken lines. They saw that a minimum of three lines would yield eight different arrangements to express the basic eight units. These are the trigrams. As each one of the eight is combined with every other one of the eight in two different ways, above or below, every possible combination of the trigrams is expressed in sixty-four different six-line hexagrams.

Like the Ennead, the elemental trigrams of the I Ching were arranged as a family of four male and four female powers. These were set along a continuum from a father figure representing Air (or Heaven), with three solid lines, to a mother figure representing Earth, with three broken lines.

The others were lined up in between, in a logical graphic sequence that will be familiar to those who know the binary system of today's computer language. This is the sequence:

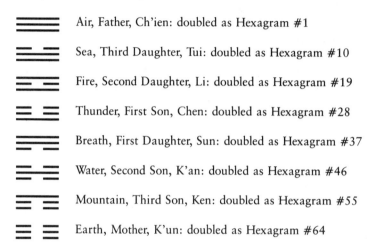

Air, Father, Ch'ien: doubled as Hexagram #1

Sea, Third Daughter, Tui: doubled as Hexagram #10

Fire, Second Daughter, Li: doubled as Hexagram #19

Thunder, First Son, Chen: doubled as Hexagram #28

Breath, First Daughter, Sun: doubled as Hexagram #37

Water, Second Son, K'an: doubled as Hexagram #46

Mountain, Third Son, Ken: doubled as Hexagram #55

Earth, Mother, K'un: doubled as Hexagram #64

Family relationships in this arrangement are significant. The eldest son and daughter stand in the center, providing a symbolic brother-sister union, like many traditional creative pairs of both East and West: Osiris-Isis, Dianus-Diana, Apollo-Artemis, Yama-Yami, Izanagi-Izanami, and so on. Curiously, each of the three "sons" has two feminine yin lines to one masculine yang line, while each of the three "daughters" has two masculine yang lines to one feminine yin line. The I Ching literature does not explain whether this was intended to represent mystic interpenetration of all elements (rendering gender distinctions illusory) or perhaps the primordial conviction that females were spiritually stronger than males.

Middle or second children stood for the other two essential elements, Fire and Water. Again, the daughter represents the element usually considered masculine, while the son represents the element usually considered feminine. In India, Persia, Greece, and other Mediterranean cultures, fire was called male and water female. According to the Tantric religion of Mother Kali, the Ocean of Blood who gave birth to the four elements as Sanskrit letters of creation magic, her "fiery" and "airy" letters were called male, her "earthy" and "watery" letters female. European alchemists in the Middle Ages preserved the same distinctions. These two elements stand at positions 3 and 6 in the eight-stage continuum, each one flanked by the secondary or intermediary powers, so every one of the four true elements is separated from every other one by at least one place. Youngest children stand next to each parent of the opposite sex, and each is secondary or intermediary in nature, like a Son-of-God bearing the parental message to the world.

Such was the ancient Chinese notion of the family of the elements. Just as the human family formed the basic unit of human society and its ordering seemed to be the model and microcosm of order in the nation and the world, so the early sages viewed the very material essences of nature as representing the cosmic order in a family-type organization. Of course, these primary matters had to be understood, the sages thought, before the cosmic scheme could be even partly revealed to the limited mortal mind. Ultimately, the aim was divination: understanding what the cosmic scheme had in store for one's own future. Yet some of the sages insisted that a full comprehension of the I Ching system contained much more than this: even a godlike knowledge of transcendent matters much greater than mere transitory human life.

2

The Fu Hsi Arrangement

Scholars of the I Ching give two basic arrangements for the sixty-four hexagrams, supposedly devised by two different Chinese culture heroes, King Wen and Fu Hsi, who was also known as Pao Hsi or Pi Hsi. Each arrangement shows every possible combination of the six lines. The arrangement usually used today is the one attributed to King Wen, a semilegendary founder of the Chou dynasty, which ruled from approximately 1100 to 250 B.C.

The main principle of King Wen's arrangement is that each pair of hexagrams forms an inverted mirror image, according to the old symbol of the heaven-mountain reflecting itself in the mirror of the abyss, like our own letters *M* (Mountain) and *W* (Water). Thus, King Wen's hexagram 4 is an upside-down image of 3; 6 is an upside-down image of 5; and so on throughout.

There are, however, four occasions where King Wen's principle of inversion doesn't work. Hexagrams 1 and 2, 27 and 28, 29 and 30, 61 and 62 don't match. Each of these eight hexagrams is top-to-bottom symmetrical, so its pattern can't be changed by standing it on its head. Instead, in these cases the pattern is changed by reversal. Solid lines in the one become broken lines in the other, and vice versa.

One might expect these four atypical pairs to be placed at significant points within the system—perhaps at the quarters or equidistant from the ends and centers. This is not done. Scholars have not been able to identify any consistent symmetry in King Wen's overall pattern, which

The King Wen Arrangement

1	2	3	4	5	6	7	8
9	10	11	12	13	14	15	16
17	18	19	20	21	22	23	24
25	26	27	28	29	30	31	32
33	34	35	36	37	38	39	40
41	42	43	44	45	46	47	48
49	50	51	52	53	54	55	56
57	58	59	60	61	62	63	64

The Fu Hsi Arrangement

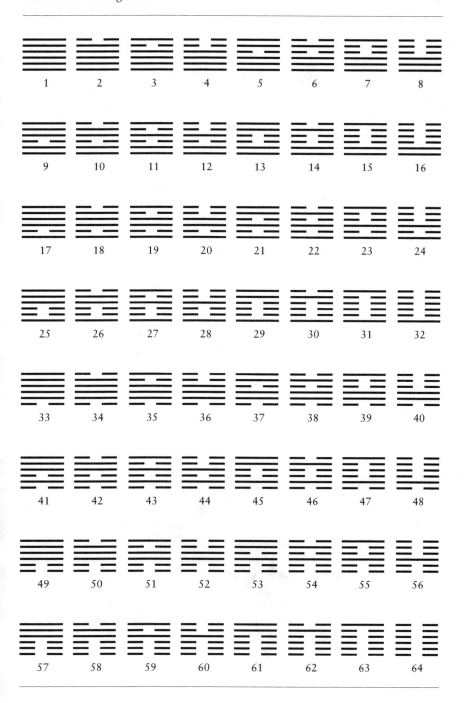

leads one to suspect that his arrangement may be a late, somewhat garbled version of an idea that was formerly self-consistent and logical throughout. Indeed, some scholars have even declared that King Wen deliberately scrambled the original order of the hexagrams, as a way of symbolizing the disarray and disorganization of the kingdom in his time.

The arrangement attributed to Fu Hsi, however, shows the overall logic that King Wen's pattern lacks. Moreover, the Fu Hsi arrangement demonstrates the very basis of all modern computer languages, the binary notation system—already worked out by the Chinese in a simple graphic form perhaps five or six thousand years ago! No one knows the true age of the Fu Hsi arrangement, but it is very old.

The seventeenth-century mathematician Gottfried Wilhelm Leibniz, father of modern calculus, was shown the Fu Hsi sequence by Joachim Bouvet, a Jesuit missionary who had worked in China. Leibniz saw that substituting a 0 for each solid line and a 1 for each broken line in this sequence would yield a perfect binary counting code. Modern computers still work on the principle of this binary code.

The Fu Hsi arrangement makes the binary code consistent not only throughout the whole sequence of sixty-four hexagrams but throughout various internal sequences also. The order of the elemental trigrams themselves, which was followed even by King Wen, illustrates the same binary counting code and may have served as a model for the whole. The same system is followed throughout upper and lower trigrams in every hexagram of the sixty-four.

To illustrate: The eight elementals are ranged from 1 to 8 as (1) Air, (2) Sea, (3) Fire, (4) Thunder, (5) Breath, (6) Water, (7) Mountain, and (8) Earth. In the Fu Hsi arrangement, the three lower lines represent Air in hexagrams 1–8, Sea in 9–16, Fire in 17–24, Thunder in 25–32, Breath in 33–40, Water in 41–48, Mountain in 49–56, and Earth in 57–64. Thus, the eight octaves or "eights" are neatly divided according to the ruling elements in their fixed sequence.

Furthermore, the same sequence is repeated in the three upper lines of each hexagram. The upper trigrams of each octave pass through the same list of elementals one at a time, in the same order. These upper trigrams, then, repeat the mystic 8, eight times over. With such internal consistencies to support Fu Hsi's pattern, one can hardly doubt that this is the original and King Wen's is a rather less elegant revision.

One of the beauties of Fu Hsi's arrangement is its inevitability. Its order not only proceeds as implacably as Fate; it also adheres throughout to an entirely logical progression that makes it easy for anyone to find any given hexagram instantly, without random searching. Every unit has its precise place in the sequence. Such a symbol system would naturally recommend itself to the Chinese love of order and "correctness."

Through the Fu Hsi arrangement, by a mathematical progression of doubles, the Book of Changes mirrors the ancient conception of nature's changes: small cycles within larger cycles, within yet larger cycles in turn, each alternating from yang to yin and back again, at varying rates of speed. Such was the ancient view of the universe originally constructed from the Great Mother's firstborn elements. Therefore the I Ching according to Fu Hsi can be viewed as a notation system for comprehending reality, just as we now assume the reality of our cosmos can be comprehended through our own systems of higher mathematics.

The progression of doubles proceeds as follows: Beginning with the top lines of all the hexagrams together, we see that these top lines alternate constantly from solid (S) to broken (B). All odd-numbered top lines are solid; all even-numbered top lines are broken; so the pattern in (1S, 1B) thirty-two times. Second lines from the top change in every second hexagram, giving a pattern of (2S, 2B) sixteen times. Third lines change every fourth hexagram: (4S, 4B) eight times. Fourth lines change every eighth hexagram: (8S, 8B) four times. Fifth lines change every sixteenth hexagram: (16S, 16B) twice. Bottom lines change only once; the first thirty-two are solid, the second thirty-two are broken. This notation system may express the "Changes" of nature's constant transformations in time and space, and every form the elements may assume within the context of such transformations.

The King Wen arrangement has no such clarity, either in its overall form or in its interpretations. By comparison to the older system, King Wen's appears muddled and arbitrary, virtually impossible to memorize, and devoid of internal logic. Its only method is the pairing of hexagrams by reversal, standing each one on its head to obtain the next. Yet even this method is inconsistently followed, since the top-to-bottom symmetrical hexagrams are inserted at random points and followed by their opposites instead of their mirror images.

There must have been a compelling reason for taking apart so nicely balanced an arrangement as Fu Hsi's, mixing it up, and destroying all its former elegance. It may well have been the same reason that led other patriarchal societies to destroy reminders of earlier matriarchal works throughout the world: to batter down temples of the Goddess despite their beauty, to burn pagan libraries despite the value of their books, to deny the sovereignty of nature despite its apparent inevitability. Like Jewish, Christian, and Islamic patriarchates, China's Confucian hierarchies attacked every aspect of the earlier culture that revered motherhood as the world-creating principle, established all family names upon the sign for "woman," and practiced sexual worship of the female power that was supposed to be the source of all mind, rationality, and inspiration.

Older Asian traditions attributed to the Goddess, not the God, every type of logical system for expressing the cycles of time and space, including calendars, time measurements by astronomical observation,

architectural and geometrical principles, numbers, poetry, and music—
which even the West still names after the Goddess as Muse.

It is significant that Fu Hsi himself was apparently not a man, but an
early god coupled with the Universal Muse, the Goddess of creation, Nu-
Kua, maker of the first human beings out of clay. Like many of her
counterparts (Ma Nu, Nun, Naunet, Mammu, Nammu, Anukis, Tiamat,
Temu, and so on), Nu-Kua was often represented as a female figure with
a fish tail. Like many other primal Goddesses, she stood for the cosmic
water womb, which Pythagoreans named the *Arché* or "first of elements."

Nu-Kua also created the four pillars that upheld the sky, establishing
the four directions, four "corners of the earth," and four elements. Her
Egyptian counterpart Nut (or Nu) also upheld the sky, which was part
of her own body, by means of the "pillars" that were her own four limbs.
Sometimes she appeared as the cosmic cow, her four legs at the corners
of the earth, her star-spotted belly forming the heaven, and her udder
producing the Milky Way, or she was a vast woman touching the earth's
corners with her feet and hands, giving birth to the sun every day.

It was said that Fu Hsi the god was a brother-consort of this primal
Goddess who brought all things into being and delegated some of her
authority to him. His legend claimed that he ruled "all under heaven"
about five thousand years ago. Like many other ancient gods of the
culture hero type, he learned from his mate the Creatress all sorts of
valuable lore that he could pass on to humanity. Western mythologies too
teem with many different versions of this divine hero.

For instance, there was the wise Hermes, who learned his wisdom as
the original Hermaphrodite joined to fish-tailed Aphrodite, another symbol of the primordial sea-womb. There was the wise Thoth, who learned
his wisdom from intimate association with the Mother of Truth, Maat or
Maa, an Egyptian name for the feminine principle of primordial "matter."
There was the wise Odin, who learned his wisdom by descending into
the womb of Mother Earth and stealing the "wise blood" stored there;
and Odin's counterpart in Asia, the wise Indra, who did the same. There
was the wise Prometheus, whose name meant Forethought and who learned
from the pre-Hellenic Libyan Wisdom-goddess Athene the same civilized
skills he taught to men.

The oldest sages and culture heroes everywhere were credited with
inspiration from the Goddess who embodied life-giving intelligence and
understanding, the primary I-dea, meaning "Goddess-within." Ancient
scriptures said nothing could be accomplished by any god without the
spirit of the Goddess. Whether she was called Minerva, Athene, Neith,
Maat, Isis, Carmenta, Kali-Maya, Shakti, Idun, Hokmah, Shekina, or
Sophia, she supplied the essential wisdom of all father gods, including
even Jehovah himself, as it was stated in Gnostic Gospels that canonical
Christianity later suppressed.

Paternalistic gods eventually forgot the maternal source of their wisdom and pretended to have created the universe on their own. This was the view set forth in writings like the Bible, where earlier images of the Goddess were assiduously omitted, buried, or declared an "abomination." The Gnostic Gospels predicted that the Goddess would punish her God for having thus neglected her and arrogantly usurped all the credit for creation, when it was she who created even him in the first place.

A similar burial of Goddess-wisdom seems to have occurred in China during the transition from an earlier Taoist system that was at least partly matriarchal, to the male-dominated Confucian hierarchy. King Wen's I Ching was obviously planned to harmonize with Confucian philosophy. It was intended for the use of kings and their advisors, who automatically assumed the character of the Superior Man, a Confucian invention often addressed by the canonical texts.

As an oracle for patriarchal rulers, the I Ching texts often sound Machiavellian, rigidly status-conscious, and greatly concerned about "firmness" and "correctness." There is a sense of toadying in the writers' anxiety to please; even unpleasant omens are said to represent "success." Commentaries on nearly every hexagram assure the ruler that progress and good fortune are certain, provided he maintains his "firm correctness." Between the lines one might glimpse the worried frowns of the king's official diviners, striving never to give the great man any offense, even when prospects look dim.

Once the overall consistency of the earlier I Ching was destroyed, seers were obliged to draw their interpretations from minute analyses of component lines, now characterized as "strong" when male (yang) and "weak" when female (yin). The former concept of equality in cyclic dualism was lost. Like its Western counterparts, Chinese society became unbalanced in favor of its males. There was, however, the inevitable backlash unwittingly brought on by the patriarchs themselves. The yin principle began to be seen as destructive to the yang, and "weak" women were thought capable of wreaking spiritual destruction on "strong" men. Logic was not the outstanding feature of patriarchal thought. In this context, one might understand how the eminently logical Fu Hsi arrangement was abandoned.

There is another mystery connected with the sexual symbolism of the hexagrams. When the entire I Ching system is founded on the idea of four elements paired (two sexes each) and contained in pictographs to the total of 4 cubed (sixty-four), why are the trigrams composed of three lines instead of four, and the hexagrams of six lines instead of eight? Triads seem oddly incongruous in this eminently eightfold realm, yet triads are its basic building blocks. Some answers may lie in very ancient Oriental trinitarian symbols, showing why the solid and broken lines were chosen to represent male and female, respectively.

The word *hexagram* does not really mean an arrangement of parallel horizontal lines. It means a geometric figure composed of two interlocking triangles: the same figure now generally accepted as a symbol of Judaism and even erroneously called the Star of David, or sometimes Solomon's Seal. In fact this figure was unknown in Jewish tradition until the twelfth century A.D., when it appeared in the symbolism of the Cabala, apparently having traveled to the mystics of Spanish Jewry from Tantric sages in the Far East, where it was known as the Sri Yantra or Great Yantra. It was not officially adopted as a Jewish emblem until five hundred years later, in the seventeenth century.

Medieval Jewish cabalists used the hexagram in much the same way as their Tantric forerunners, to represent divinity in terms of a union of the sexes. They even claimed that the hexagram first appeared inside the Ark of the Covenant, along with the tablets of the laws, and that it stood for male and female deities in perpetual sexual intercourse, the same meaning it bore in India. To cabalists, the union of God and his Shekina (the Female Principle) was modeled on the union of Shiva and the cosmic Goddess, Kali-Shakti, his mother-sister-bride, who also devoured him and gave him eternal cyclic rebirth.

Cabalists envisioned the Shekina in much the same way as early Gnostic sages envisioned Jehovah's spouse Sophia, who embodied his wisdom and the essential spirit that enabled him to function at all. She too was a Westernized version of the Tantric Shakti. Cabalists claimed that all the world's evil arose from God's separation from this female principle and the purpose of a true sage was to put God and his empowering female spirit back together. The usual route toward this end was sex magic, also designed according to the Tantric model.

Such ideas were shown in graphic shorthand by the double-triadic hexagram—the original source of the three solid (male) and three broken (female) lines. The six lines of the I Ching's components represented a hexagram taken apart, in a special analytic way, according to one of the world's oldest symbolic representations of the cosmic Goddess and her methods of creation.

Here's how it worked.

The original triangle stood for the Goddess's trinity of Creator, Preserver, and Destroyer, she of the thousand names, such as Maya the birth-giving Virgin, Durga the preserving Mother, and Kali Ma the death-dealing Crone. Her primary symbol was a downward-pointing triangle, the Yoni Yantra, sometimes called Kali Yantra. This represented a vulva (Sanskrit *yoni*), and femaleness in general: by extension, a womb, motherhood, female sexuality, the life spirit embodied in menstrual blood, or the world-activating power of the Goddess herself. The same symbol stood for "woman" and "Goddess" among ancient Egyptians, pre-Hellenic Greeks, Tantric Buddhists, and the gypsies who migrated westward from Hindustan.

The primordial female triangle became a male-female hexagram by eight stages, graphically represented as follows.

At first there was only the Goddess alone, containing within herself all the elements in a fluid, unformed state (Fig. 1). With the passage of ages and by her will, eventually a spark of life was formed within her core, represented by a dot (Fig. 2). Tantric sages called this spark the *bindu*, and one of the Goddess's titles was Bindumati, Mother of the Bindu. Among Cabalists it became Bina, the Womb of Earth.

Figure 1   Figure 2

The bindu grew and slowly became a separate being within the Mother (Fig. 3), though it still lay wholly inside her borders. At this early stage of the divine creation, the sages said, darkness (the god) was still enveloped in a greater Darkness (his Mother). The god was still one with the author of his being, Maha-Kali, the Great Power.

At the fourth stage, the god was born. Represented by an upward-pointing triangle—which often also symbolized the masculine principle of fire—the god broke through the boundaries of the primordial maternal triangle (Fig. 4). Here, at the moment of "birth," the idea of the male deity was conveyed by three solid lines, while that of female deity became three broken lines. Thus was the design taken apart, and its components utilized as trigrams and hexagrams in the I Ching.

Figure 3   Figure 4

In allowing her boundaries to be penetrated from within by an emerging Other, the Goddess demonstrated her true creativity. She became the universal Mother. This crucial moment of birth was synonymous with creation, according to the ancient concept. This was the moment when the Goddess (not the emerging God) said, "Let there be light," because the eyes of her newborn first perceived the light of existence, as he himself might become the light of fire or the sun. In the classical world, the Goddess had names like Juno Lucina or Diana Lucifera, the Bringer of Light. From her the biblical Yahweh copied his *Fiat lux.*

The god's birth was celebrated each year at midwinter. The nocturnal festival was known as the Night of the Mother to pre-Christian Britons, which may explain why Christmas Eve (the time of actual birth) carried even more significance in Old England than Christmas Day. In Alexandria, the god's birth was hailed by joyful shouts: "The Virgin (Kore) has given birth! The light grows!" The naked image of the divine birth-giving Virgin was decorated with gold stars and carried seven times around the temple.

Just as, in pagan belief, creation was a birth, so every birth was a new creation. Each year the Aeon or year-god was reborn from the eternally virgin, eternally maternal Goddess. Thus, at the mystic point of creation itself, the graphic symbol of the Mother became three broken lines, while that of her son-spouse was three solid lines.

Male and female triangles, once separated, came together again in a very ancient figure that later rounded off to the mathematical sign of infinity in so-called Arabic numerals, which were actually Hindu in origin. The two tangential circles or teardrop shapes of this sign meant the same as two tangential triangles: the two sexes in contact (Fig. 5). The female triangle above now took on the aspect of a nourishing breast, while the male received her nourishment.

This was also taken as a sexual sign, in unconscious but nevertheless real recognition of the connection between adult sexuality and the bond between mother and infant. According to Tantric symbolism, the female triangle was placed above the male, who then assumed all forms of relationship with her: offspring, twin, spouse, and eventually sacrificial victim, as he became the eternally dying-and-reborn god, similar to Osiris, Attis, Dionysus, Adonis, Orpheus, Yama, and so on. Therefore Tantric yogis and their shaktis (priestesses) favored female-superior sexual positions, which Vedic and Confucian patriarchs condemned because of their association with the Old Religion that they wanted to erase. Though this style of lovemaking was instituted by Shiva as Universal God and the original "daughters of the sages" (shaktis), patriarchal Brahman priests insisted that it was a perversion.

However, Tantric yogis continued to hold that sexual union in true love was an intimation of divinity, giving the partners a sense of merging "like the pouring of water into water" Fig. 6). Similarly in Egypt, the Goddess and her god were represented by vessels of water, their conjunction by combination of the two waters, as in the sacred talisman known as *menat.* In the Middle East, a sacrificial god was preceded by a vessel of water in procession to his place of execution, a tradition that was followed even in

Figure 5

Figure 6

the story of Jesus (Mark 14:13). Like Shiva, the Christian God also was born of the same Mother on whom, as divine spouse, he begot himself.

By penetrating each other to the farthest boundary, god and Goddess formed between them the ancient Tantric symbol of the world and also the yoni: a diamond (Fig. 7), flanked by four new triangles that were assimilated to the elements, the four directions, the four corners of the earth (when the earth was supposed to be square), the four winds, the four divisions of the zodiac, the four Sons of Horus, or the Norsemen's related spirits of north, east, south, and west that upheld the heavens. Sometimes this symbol represented a family or clan. All these ideas could be expressed in a simple glyph of six lines.

Figure 7

Figure 8

Finally, the ultimate interpenetration was shown by the full hexagram (Fig. 8). Male and female principles extended even beyond each other's boundaries, becoming "one" in sixfold symmetry. This was the union proposed by cabalists as well as Tantric sages: the symbol of eternal conception and re-creation. This was the hidden reason for the rabbinic traditions claiming that the Ark of the Covenant contained male and female images sexually joined, "in the form of a hexagram," and that the triple six of Solomon's golden talents (1 Kings 10:14)

represented the king's sexual union with his goddess, who gave him his great wisdom.

This explains also the early Christians' horror of the sixfold symbol of Aphrodite, similarly united with Hermes as the first "hermaphrodite," and their insistence that three sixes made a devilish number (666) and six was "the number of sin." However, such sexual joining was envisioned for the male-female Primal Androgyne common to ancient India, Persia, Greece, and Rome. Even Jewish patriarchs declared that Adam and Eve were androgynously united in one body until God separated them.

The ultimate absorption of the god into the Yoni Yantra (Goddess) was his immolation, usually conceived as a voluntary sacrifice of his life for the salvation of the earthly world, which needed the life-force inherent in divine blood. As Kali the Destroyer, the Goddess devoured her consort and returned to the original solitary female form of the Yantra (Fig. 1). Thus the cycles of creation and destruction were carried on throughout the life of the universe.

Such were the secret meanings of the classic hexagram and possibly also of the I Ching hexagrams. Their sacredness may have begun with the "moment of birth" design (Fig. 4) revered in the East. Why else would male and female principles have been represented by such curiously abstract markings? Elsewhere, they were usually recognizably genital signs, such as the Hindu lingam and yoni; or the cross and orb; or the Tau and loop such as shown on the Egyptian *ankh*; or the spear and cauldron of Celtic symbolism, which also appeared in medieval romances as sword and stone; or the wand and cup, Paschal candle and baptismal font, unicorn and enclosed garden of Christian iconography. Such extreme attenuation of male-female symbolism as the I Ching presents is surely an indication of a high order of rigidly controlled asceticism, typical of intensely patriarchal societies.

Yet everything in human communication begins with some perception of relationship, however farfetched it may seem. Alphabetical letters and number signs are based on the sacred pictographs of antiquity. Throughout the world, such pictographs were commonly attributed to the primal Goddess. Even the letters of our own alphabet were said to have been invented by the ancient Latin Goddess Carmenta, who also devised sacred poems and magic songs (*carmen*, charms). Although a god-hero like Fu Hsi, Prometheus, Evander, Garuda, or Thoth may have carried the inventions to earth dwellers, he was essentially a messenger of the Goddess, his mother-bride.

Of course symbol systems are not really invented by deities. They are invented by human beings. It is the creation and transmission of symbol systems that most clearly distinguishes humans from other animals. Probably there never was a real Fu Hsi, any more than there was a real Hermes or Thoth. The story that the Goddess gave the I Ching to the culture hero points to the likelihood that this symbol system—like other systems of ideograms, numbers, calendars, alphabets, measurements, and hiero-glyphics—was originated by women in a matriarchal age, when men served chiefly as hunters, warriors, and field hands while women evolved the more civilized skills.

As in prehistoric Scandinavia the secrets of runic writing belonged solely to women, and in Babylon it was the priestesses who knew the secrets of cuneiform writing, so also in prepatriarchal China the art of making signs on paper used to be a feminine art. If the legend of Fu Hsi is as old as has been supposed, then it would place the invention of the original I Ching in this matriarchal period.

This conclusion is also suggested by the legend of Fu Hsi's birth from a virgin mother, the Goddess's earthly birthgiving incarnation, impreg-nated by a divine white elephant whom Hindus called Ganesha and Hebrews called Behemoth. This deity's original name meant "Lord of Hosts." The Chinese virgin mother was Moye, derived from the Hindu Maya (Buddha's virgin mother), who was also Greek Maia, Syrian Mara, Hebrew Mary. The life of Fu Hsi repeated the same cyclic pattern of other elder gods returning always to their female source, the eternal Queen of Heaven who was both Bride and Mother, when the seasons of the god's birth, marriage, and death in relation to her were symbolically enacted each year.

The cyclic nature of the I Ching indicates feminine origins. A philoso-phy of universal periodicity characterized matrifocal societies, probably reflecting the periodicity of feminine existence itself. Patriarchal societies tended to see both life and time as linear, with hierarchical categories and the We/They kind of thinking that typifies warlike male-dominated groups, and is always essential to waging war on others.

Thus it may be appropriate for women to reclaim the I Ching and look beyond the late addition of its Confucian confusions, returning to the simplicity and consistency of the original. The hexagrams' traditional interpretations suggest many interesting internal progressions, perhaps left over from the earlier arrangement. The system seems even more discursive than its patriarchal commentators imagined. Though they al-ways tried to read the will of Mother Nature in its bare, abstract lines, they may have missed much simply because they were deficient in the perception of connections and relationships that the feminine mind tends to master easily. Any divinatory system needs free, uninhibited play of the imagination and the unconscious, which is not usually possible for a system that has been harnessed to the service of kings. Matriarchs gen-erally left room for individualism, metaphor, and poetry. In a sense, the I Ching may be seen as a poem of being.

3

The Meanings
of Divination

The traditional method of consulting the I Ching is a rather complicated process of repeatedly sorting, arranging, and counting certain subdivisions of a group of fifty yarrow sticks, in three separate stages, over and over, to determine each line of a basic hexagram, plus the "changing" lines to produce a second, contrasting hexagram for additional illumination. Probably this method was invented by court diviners long ago, in order to draw out the time required for a consultation, to impress the questioner with fancy manual flourishes and intricate manipulations, and to give themselves an air of great learning, by which they were enabled to master so complex a system in the first place.

These elegant manipulations of the yarrow sticks built up, line by line, a pair of hexagrams that would provide—both individually and in combination—a reply to any given query. This same purpose is more easily achieved by other methods, however. These other methods are given below, because they are much simpler than the yarrow stick numbering, need no special equipment, require no extensive practice, and yet yield the same results.

One of the simplest ways to build up a hexagram is the three-coin method, which was also popular among the Chinese. Three coins are tossed together six times into the air and allowed to fall on a flat surface. Each time, they will show one of four possible arrangements: three heads, three tails, two heads and a tail, or two tails and a head.

Each toss establishes one line of two different hexagrams, a primary hexagram and a secondary hexagram, which are drawn side by side on paper as the coin tossing proceeds. Both drawings begin with the bottom line and continue upward, ending with the top line. Here is how the coins determine the two hexagrams:

	Primary Hexagram	Secondary Hexagram
3 heads	Solid line	Solid line
3 tails	Broken line	Broken line
2 heads, 1 tail	Solid line	Broken line
2 tails, 1 head	Broken line	Solid line

The latter two are known as changing lines, which means they can alter their character because one of the coins is the opposite of the other two. Thus, the primary line is penetrated by its opposite, like the swirled circles of the yang-and-yin symbol. When these changing lines are altered, an entirely different hexagram naturally results.

This secondary hexagram is to be read after the primary one and in conjunction with it, so the two are presumed to influence one another. In a sense, certain lines of action or attitude indicated by one of them will bring about effects indicated by the other. In this way the reading can take on surprising twists at times and can become complex, depending on how interaction between the two hexagrams is perceived.

As an alternative to drawing the hexagrams on paper, one may lay down lengths of cord or string: a straight piece for each solid line, a piece knotted in the middle for each broken line. Outdoors, lines can be drawn on the ground with a pointed object, or even formed of twigs or grass blades. A personal set of "magic sticks" can be made out of any handy materials: wood, wire, or plastic rods, pieces of dowel, pencils, chopsticks, toothpicks, matches, tongue depressors, or any other straight sticks, some painted a different color in the center to represent the broken lines. A full set would require a maximum of twenty-four sticks, twelve of each type.

It is quite likely that the original yarrow sticks used by the ancient Chinese were actually laid down as direct graphic representations of the hexagrams themselves, rather than sorted and added as a numerical tool for determining straight and broken lines. Divinatory "rods" or wands were common in the ancient Middle East and even in medieval Europe, where perpetrators of crimes were supposed to be discovered by "casting the rods" on the altar of a church. Therefore, those who like to manipulate real objects as an aid to meditation may be assured of a genuinely archaic tradition about "magic sticks" that might imbue such objects with a sense of mana. In the same way, the mana of accumulated centuries of use can invest such divinatory objects as Tarot cards, whose symbolism has so many ramifications in ancient tradition.

Not only cards, but also dice, dice boards, and other board games have always been popular tools of divination and religious instruction in the Orient. Unlike Westerners, the people of the East did not consider such things frivolous or sinful distractions. On the contrary, they believed in teaching children or illiterates the principles of religion and philosophy by means of games that they could enjoy. Game players could study pictures of the deities on their boards or cards and grasp their attributes, or the ideas they stood for, in the very process of play. Dice made of wood, bone, or ivory have served many purposes through the centuries, not the least of which was divination. Indeed, the prophetic Urim and Thummim mentioned in the Bible were thought to have been divinatory dice.

Therefore, dice may serve as well as coins for establishing the hexagrams of the I Ching. Three dice are tossed and allowed to roll to a stop. Then, the numbers on their upper surfaces are read. Chances of odd or even numbers are the same as the chances of heads or tails among the three coins. They are presumed to establish the lines of the hexagrams in the same way, from the bottom line to the top line:

	Primary Hexagram	Secondary Hexagram
3 odd numbers	Solid line	Solid line
3 even numbers	Broken line	Broken line
2 odd, 1 even	Solid line	Broken line
2 even, 1 odd	Broken line	Solid line

Odd numbers on the dice are equated with solid lines, like the coins' heads, because the first hexagram is made entirely of solid lines and all odd-numbered top lines are solid throughout the entire Fu Hsi arrangement. Even numbers on the dice are equated with broken lines, like the coins' tails, because the sixty-fourth hexagram is made entirely of broken lines and all even-numbered top lines are broken.

Because of their antiquity, the use of dice is appropriate to the study of the I Ching. So is the use of a special board to throw the dice on. Our basic board for the games of chess and checkers may even have a remote connection with the I Ching. Both chess and checkers are very old games, of fundamentally unknown origin although it is usually assumed that they were Oriental. Chess was found in India at an early date, checkers even earlier in ancient Egypt and eastward. The board of sixty-four squares, divided into eight rows and eight columns, serves for both of these games. It can serve equally well as a grounding board for the Fu Hsi arrangement of the I Ching.

To turn a chessboard into an I Ching board, it is only necessary to draw the hexagrams in order on its sixty-four squares, one to each square. Each octave fits neatly into its own row (or column), and a number of interesting cross-references can be seen in the way hexagrams relate in the other direction.

To pick out a hexagram or two for contemplation, a single die can be tossed onto the board, to choose whatever square it happens to light upon. Or, one may close one's eyes and place a finger, or some other pointer, on the board at random. As the Tibetans do with their popular game of Rebirth, one can even play a game on the I Ching board and read interpretations from the passage of pieces over the squares. An especially meaningful hexagram might be determined, for instance, from the last square on which a king is found at the end of a chess game.

A certain playful attitude is not at all inappropriate to the use of divinatory materials, since that is not only a time-honored tradition but also one of the best ways to develop the creative openness of mind that elicits insightful ideas from the wellsprings of the unconscious. One might even play with different combinations of the common divinatory methods, creating new kinds of games as well as new associations of ideas.

When the Fu Hsi arrangement is followed, the coin or dice methods of creating hexagrams are just as easy to use as the chessboard method. Unlike King Wen's hexagrams, Fu Hsi's are quickly located in the sequence. The lower three lines of any given hexagram instantly reveal which octave the hexagram occupies. Needing no memorization of symbols at all, Fu Hsi's arrangement is even simpler to read than an ordinary numerical system, once one grasps the principle of the binary code on which it is based.

Many have found it fascinating to meditate on the hexagrams and study their commentaries—not because they believe this or any other divinatory system can actually foretell the future, in the simplistic sense, but because the allegorical meanings suggested by the system can contribute fresh insights to any situation. Thus, the I Ching may quite possibly lead to creative solutions to any problems. This is perhaps the true value of such ancient modes of thought.

As a set of allegories, founded in universal psychological archetypes, the images suggested by the hexagrams represent a new way of looking at any particular circumstances. Just as it is generally useful to consider alternate opinions on any puzzling or disturbing matters, so it may be useful to allow a divinatory system to suggest alternative views. Even when new suggestions so derived may seem irrelevant at first, further thought may reveal a hidden but meaningful connection in one's own attitudes. Insight can be obtained from the I Ching, as from Tarot cards or any other aids to private contemplation, as well as from another person who presents a differing viewpoint. Like the unconscious material that can sometimes surface in dreams, these images can yield additional understanding to the person who plays with them, juxtaposes them, and considers them in the light of those universal keys to the secret mind, myth and symbol.

Therefore, ancient systems of divination like the I Ching need not be dismissed as meaningless superstitions. For many intelligent individuals, such systems can serve a useful purpose in providing clarification and advice—at a tiny fraction of the cost demanded by other kinds of advisors. If the system "feels right," seems to make some kind of sense, and points the way to a fresh outlook on anything, then it is surely helpful enough to be worth using.

Hexagram Location Chart
According to the Fu Hsi Arrangement

		Upper Trigram							
		Ch'ien Air	Tui Sea	Li Fire	Chen Thunder	Sun Breath	K'an Water	Ken Mountain	K'un Earth
Lower Trigram	Ch'ien Air	1	2	3	4	5	6	7	8
	Tui Sea	9	10	11	12	13	14	15	16
	Li Fire	17	18	19	20	21	22	23	24
	Chen Thunder	25	26	27	28	29	30	31	32
	Sun Breath	33	34	35	36	37	38	39	40
	K'an Water	41	42	43	44	45	46	47	48
	Ken Mountain	49	50	51	52	53	54	55	56
	K'un Earth	57	58	59	60	61	62	63	64

To relieve the confusion of the King Wen hexagrams, some diviners created chessboardlike charts, with upper trigrams placed along the top edge and lower trigrams placed along the side edge. Such a chart made the search easier, since the number of each hexagram could be placed where the appropriate row and column came together. When hexagrams of the King Wen arrangement are so charted, the numbers appear at arbitrary positions in the diagram without any obvious relationship to one another. However, when the Fu Hsi arrangement is charted, the perhaps surprising result is that all the rows show correct consecutive numbering from left to right, 1 through 64.

Such precision actually makes the chart unnecessary, since one always knows where to find any given hexagram immediately in the Fu Hsi system. But a chart is given here as a matter of interest, to show a final proof of the logical consistency of the older I Ching of the Goddess.

≡≡≡

4

The First Octave (Ch'ien)

This is the realm of Air, also called Sky, Highest, Zenith, Heaven, Authority, Father, or Spirit. Most images of the paternal god, or Father Heaven, are associated with the element of Air, usually manifested to earthly senses as breath or wind. Ancient writers like Diogenes of Apollonia said that the spirit of God is nothing more than air constantly drawn into the body as breath and that it permeates all things, as air can penetrate everywhere.

As an element, air was identified with spirituality, the invisible, or the supernatural, including ghosts or other kinds of disembodied souls, and the creatures of heaven—especially birds, often believed to be souls of the dead. Patriarchal writers claimed that their god breathed life into the world or spoke a creative Word (Logos) with the air of his breath, which magically brought the universe into being. Thus the male creative principle was held to replace the female creative principle of mother-blood. Male gods, by definition unable to give birth, could yet claim parenthood of living things by infusing them with their air element. In like manner, patriarchal Brahman fathers pretended to give life to newborn children by breathing in their faces.

Worshipers of male gods also confidently expected their own airy souls to be taken back to the lofty realm of their origin in heaven, where the Father lived, surrounded by winged attendants. Then each spirit could live as free as a bird, no longer weighed down by the onerous demands of the flesh. Mystics enlarged upon these heavenly conditions: one could fly like the wind, soar like a cloud, walk invisibly on the earth, ascend to the dazzling sphere of the sun. To live as a spirit of the air sounded grand. So, naturally, men embraced doctrines that dangled the promise before them.

The gods who made such promises were vaguely located at the zenith or the top of the sky, or else at the summit of a holy mountain. Therefore, all things were "under" such a god, who was accordingly seen as the ruler of all the rest of the pyramid. Well-known examples are Zeus, Jupiter, Ahura Mazda, Ra, or Jehovah.

Earth was the base and foundation of the whole structure; therefore, her element occupied the eighth octave of the I Ching. Fu Hsi's arrangement progresses in logical sequence through the cosmic order, arranging the elements according to increasing density. The Chinese envisioned the first octave of Air as an embodiment of pure yang (masculine principle), while the eighth octave of Earth, at the other end of the continuum, embodied yin, the feminine. However, it was not until the late development of patriarchal thought that the first was considered intrinsically superior to the second. Thus it would be equally valid to picture the sequence all on the same horizontal level, extending from right to left.

Air ≡≡≡≡
over
Air ≡≡≡≡

1. Heaven, Air, Sky, Authority (Ch'ien)

The element of Air was seen as the spirit of the sky god, or Father Heaven, whose Western names Zeus, Jupiter, Deus, Divus, and so on were derived from Sanskrit Dyaus Pitar. As the Greek writers believed air was the invisible, universal god-soul penetrating and animating all things, so also the Chinese believed their sky god Shang-Te could live in, and as, the air. This sky god was also known as the August Personage of Jade, a consort of the Earth Mother Kuan-Yin.

The influence of the airy-heaven god could be a problem, in that men might think they could imitate his loftiness and so commit the sin of hubris. This may have been a new attitude, designed to contradict those sages who called God a figment of the human mind, a projection of the Self into an impersonal heaven. Having made God in their own image, men began to fear their creation as they also feared the uncontrollable or reprehensible aspects of themselves.

The first hexagram was often taken as a solar symbol, the dragon chariot in an open space. This was considered propitious. The six solid lines were sometimes called the six dragons. The Chinese associated the dragon with good fortune, righteousness, the airs of heaven, the zenith, healing, and godlike glory. The dragon chariot may be said to resemble the Tarot card of worldly success and glory, the Chariot, which was drawn by the black-and-white horses or sphinxes of night and day.

This hexagram indicated righteous laws, worthwhile goals, or godlike strengths. Useful, inspiring, noble endeavors, dedicated to the betterment of society, would win success. However, one must guard against hubris or excessive pride.

In Western Gnostic and Mithraic traditions, the gate of heaven was guarded by the paternal figure called Pater, Petra, Peter, or Pater Patrum (Father of Fathers). He judged the airy souls, to determine whether they were worthy of admittance to the paradise among the stars. Fourth-century Roman Christians corrupted his title to Papa (Pope) and applied it to their own bishop, but the Petra or Peter was really the same as Rome's former pagan Janus, the "janitor" (gatekeeper) of heaven. The gatekeeper controlled even the savior-son figure, to whom he could deny admittance through the heavenly gate, until the time was ripe. This may have influenced the Christian legend about Peter's thrice-repeated denial of Jesus.

Denial of the son by the Pater was also an Oedipal myth. Gates and doorways were common female genital symbols; thus the Mother's "gate of heaven" was guarded by the *Pater* against the *Filius*. Temple gates, also called gates of heaven, used to be marked with obvious female signs, such as the *vesica piscis, sheila-na-gig*, omega/horseshoe, cowrie shell, or yoni. To enter the gate of paradise was to be sexually/maternally welcomed by the Goddess, whose abstracted image persisted behind the overtly masculine guardians, like Peter, imperiously demanding credentials. In most symbolic systems, the true paradise remained the Mother's "garden" even when she was suppressed and removed from the theological mainstream. She was hidden in the sky as Queen of Heaven.

Sea
over
Air

2. *Resolution* (Kuai)

This hexagram traditionally called for frank discussion of any important issues, with firm resolve not to lose sight of ultimate goals. A sincere appeal for support would be advantageous. Every difficulty should be brought out into plain sight, for concealment would only mean additional trouble.

Placement of the Sea or Deep over airy heaven means hidden matters will be brought into the light of day. The commentaries equate this with displacement, since the normal order of things obviously sets the sky above the sea. However, this upside-down arrangement brings forth buried truths, as any displacement in the usual course of events is likely to do. Without traditional guidance, one proceeds "slowly and with difficulty" toward the resolution that is needed for new insights.

Commentators said firmness of purpose will bring success. Resolution and willingness to undertake hard, goal-oriented work are the keys to a beneficial end, which might be symbolized by an alternate version of the entrance-to-paradise image. This image set a sign of the Sea Mother high in the air and also made heaven accessible only to persons of great moral strength and unflagging resolution, willing to suffer enormous difficulties for the sake of the goal.

This was the golden city in the sky, atop the highest, most inaccessible of earth's pinnacles. It was attainable only by the rainbow bridge, conceived as the veil or necklace of the Goddess, whereby men might ascend to comprehension of her true nature, for rainbows were seen in many forms of her waters. Hindus said all earthly appearances were the "rainbow veils" of her spirit. Northern Aryans called the rainbow the Goddess' ornament, Brisingamen, but Odin's warrior cult renamed it Bifrost, the rainbow bridge to the soldier's Valhalla.

Persian Aryans too surrounded the golden paradise with dangers that only a great hero could overcome. Their rainbow bridge, called the Kinvad, had a razor's edge, so that weak or sinful persons would be cut to pieces when trying to cross it. Like most patriarchs, the inventors of this idea disliked excessive aspiration in others, which might lead to loss of their own jealously held positions. They said their gods would punish hubris or overaspiration, but neither god nor man ever defined the line between reprehensible hubris and laudable ambition.

Some said it was evil for men to want to become immortal or godlike. This was Adam's offense in desiring the fruit of the Tree of (eternal) Life. However, all the Mystery religions including Christianity held out to mortals a divine promise of that very thing.

Fire
over
Air

3. *Wealth, Great Possessions* (Ta Yu)

In the realm of the heaven god, possessions were seen as unequivocally good and desirable, for the specific concept of private property seems to have begun with patriarchy. Supreme success, good fortune, and the acquisition of wealth were equated with the god's blessings, given in return for rich presents offered to him. His worshipers apparently believed that he craved acquisitions, just as they did. A great wagon loaded with valuable things is mentioned in the commentaries. Through ascending fires, princes make offerings to heaven.

Wealth and possessions mean earthly power. Though a display of majesty is indicated, fortunate folk must try not to appear too proud and not to forget that appropriate proportions of their gains must be set aside for thank offerings.

Fire high in the air also suggests flashing jewels held up to admiration, especially rubies, as well as the glad sunlight, a noontide of prosperity—in effect, the ever-desired place in the sun.

A sunny climate is suggested by ten palm trees, which may be likened to the mention in Gnostic texts of the Ten Trees of the Treasure House of Light, meaning the ten fingers of Sophia, Mother of Wisdom. Gnostic thinkers talked more of the treasure of wisdom than of material things. They said wisdom was the only treasure that could never be lost, stolen, or corrupted by time or by human wickedness. Therefore, the Superior Man (or woman) should assiduously acquire as much knowledge and wisdom as possible. These are great possessions indeed.

Thunder
over
Air

4. *Power, Greatness*

(Ta Chuang)

Wealth (hexagram 3) leads on to power (hexagram 4) as a natural cause and effect, in view of human acquisitiveness and the usual attitude of awe toward the wealthy.

Thunder in the air is a supreme symbol of godlike power, as seen in Western tradition through such figures as Zeus the Thunderer or Thor (Thunder) the Mighty. What such a powerful deity says is heard everywhere, since no voice speaks louder than thunder.

Thunder is likened to the energy that mounts up toward heaven, also, challenging the higher powers and perhaps bringing down the wrath of a greater deity. Mythology speaks of occasions when the Great Goddess used her lightning-arrow, like Diana Lucifera, to chastise the hubris of her upstart virgin-born son the god and cast him back down to the earth.

Great power demands equally great care to do what is right, because the most powerful being is the center of attention. Power alone may not indicate strength of character. Rather, it may function as a test of character for those of wide influence.

The would-be wielder of the thunderbolt in his airy chariot was associated with mythic figures like that of Phaethon or Tesup, mortal or semimortal heroes who aspired to godhood. Their myths probably descended from ancient sacrificial ceremonies, when men were actually identified as Sons of God and sacrificed to their heavenly fathers, with whom they subsequently merged. The oldest ceremonies were conducted by priestesses of the Goddess, representing the Fate who decreed all births and deaths, even those of gods. In the guise of Nemesis or "Retribution" she could govern even the greatest wielder of the thunderbolt, and send his golden sun chariot down into the western sea every day.

Breath
over
Air

5. *Clouds, Small*
Nurture (Hsaio Kuo)

In this hexagram, former power suffers a diminution under frustrating clouds that are thick but bring no nourishing rain. Former power becomes shadowy, less obvious. Stronger, positive forces should be held back for a time. Gentleness and restraint are required. Skill should replace aggressive activity.

The symbol of breath or wind over heaven refers to the power of hazy, restrained elements in a situation where they may be very hard to see. Breath blends with, and disappears into the air. Nonetheless, it is essential to life. One must pay attention to what seems invisible.

As the powerful might become overly arrogant and make mistakes, so this hexagram warns against excessive complacency and counsels the reining in of ambitious drives when events indicate. Sensitivity can be more important than ambition when movement needs to be curtailed.

In the midst of dark clouds, a man minutely studies his small pot of golden treasure, perhaps seeking a key to the Pearly Gates shown in an Egyptianized version. The opening is guarded by the Two Ladies (Buto and Nekhbet), each within an arch of fourteen pearls, like the fourteen nights of Osiris's journey into the dark and his ascension. The gate is forbidden. The supplicant remains outside unless there is an increase in understanding, sensitivity, and awareness of things outside the sharp focus on small, material gains. Everything here is narrow, compact, indrawn, and hedged about by the clouds.

Water
over
Air

6. *Waiting, Calculated Inaction* (Hsu)

Water over air indicates that the clouds will rise slowly, holding their nourishing rain until the proper or preordained time, no matter how urgently the rain is needed. Forces of time and change can't be hurried.

No matter how hard it may be to hold back and wait, no action should be taken until circumstances are clarified and a course of action can be more plainly seen. Lurking threats in the clouds may destroy the reckless. Doubts must be held in abeyance. Inactivity must not be allowed to erode confidence.

Such obviously sequential references as the ones shown here, in traditional interpretations of hexagrams 5, 6, and 7, make it clear that the Fu Hsi arrangement had a continuous story to tell, which was later disrupted by changes in the order of symbols.

Water precedes air as the first environment of the inactive fetal entity waiting for the proper time to be born. Accordingly, ancient myths of creation postulated primordial conditions of water and darkness, ordered by the unseen hand of the Mother. In her own good time, she guided the new world or the new being toward a first experience of light.

Matriarchal cyclic traditions said the new was also the old. The corpse could be remade in the uterine darkness, to be reborn or reincarnated. Possibly such ideas actually began with the observation that stillborn infants resemble those dead in old age of wasting disease. Both the corpse and the fetus were supposed to dwell in a waiting state, while unseen changes silently impelled both toward a new state of being. Such progress could never be hurried. It would come only in the fullness of time and by the hand of Mother Nature.

Mountain
over
Air

7. Energy, Great Nurture (Ta Ch'u)

Waiting generates potential energy. This hexagram represents a buildup of power and insight for eventual movement. Sky-scraping mountains appear motionless but are not. Their snows and rocks may begin violent, irresistible movement at any time.

Heaven in the midst of a mountain recalls the common Asiatic image of the gods' paradise, located on the highest peaks ("Himalaya" means heaven). All deities reposed in the lap of the Goddess Mother of the Universe, Chomo-Lung-Ma, whose Western name is Everest. Nurtured by her, the gods renewed their powers and received the maternal *karuna* (love) that gave them their divine energy.

On earth, energy can be stored by organization of resources. Power accompanied by restraint arouses the image of a fine mountain-bred horse galloping under rein. The traditions also say that eating should not be done in the home place, meaning best results in eventual action will be gained by an outgoing attitude, sensitive to the nurture of others as well as one's self.

Power accompanied by restraint also suggested the irresistible movements of birth when the buildup of energy and the time of inward nurture attain completion. Maternal support of the offspring created from the hidden maternal blood continued after the time of birth, in all-important rituals of eating. Men were naturally awed by women's mysterious ability to give life and nurture from their own bodies. Thus, naturally, the universalized principle of nurture was attributed to the supreme Goddess.

Tantric and Taoist (prepatriarchal) sources asserted that energy and activity were intrinsic attributes of females, while passivity was characteristic of males, who required stimulation from an outside source before they could function. This view, based on the idea of female-as-mother and male-as-child, diametrically opposed the male-female imagery of Western patriarchy. Yet common to both traditions was the concept of the World Egg, holding all things in potential or latent movement while receiving nurture from the Mother—herself egg-shaped when she assumed the guise of creatress and pregnant source from which all life would emerge.

Earth over Air

8. *Peace* (T'ai)

The inferior departs. The superior is approaching. The first octave ends quietly with all things in union and prospering, ruled by harmony, accord, order, and benevolence.

The nurturing female principle is in ascendancy over male aggression, which is therefore properly controlled. Mother Earth hates warfare and will not allow it in her time of burgeoning, as at the beginning of spring. The environment is cooperative at this time.

One commentary says the wall of defense has crumbled back into the moat, indicating no more need for defenses. The earth peacefully reabsorbs all things.

Heeding the advice of previous hexagrams, one may come to terms with temptations to misuse power or to oppress others. The result is peace. All parts of the whole may finally work together harmoniously toward higher goals.

Archetypal myths depict the infantile period—when nature was controlled by the seemingly all-powerful mother—as a kind of paradise, to which men hoped to return after death. Egyptian funerary charms insisted that the divine pharoahs would live after death at the Mother's breast and would never again be weaned. Her maternal figure was painted inside the lids of sarcophagi, reaching down to embrace the deceased and carry him to her bosom. This image was later adopted but made irrational by Christian claims of eternal rest in a nonnurturant male bosom, that of Abraham or Jesus.

Psychologists have recognized hidden but intense male envy of female nurturant functions and the secret jealousy of the adult male displaced by a new infant rival. Such jealousy became destructive of the peace fostered by the primitive mothers.

5

The Second Octave (Tui)

This octave covers the element of water as experienced by earthly senses, in the form of Sea, also variously defined as Lake, Abyss, Marsh, Pit, Deep, and similar images of water forming an interface between the lowest depths and the sky above.

The power of water to reflect the heavens, like a mirror, led ancient thinkers to view bodies of water as the means of bringing heavenly splendor down to earth. To bathe in waters illuminated by the sky was to immerse one's self in the light of heaven and to gain life-giving energy.

Sea was called the youngest daughter, standing next to the Air father to form a pair of opposites, as the youngest female in any family would be opposite to the eldest male in both sex and age. Depths would naturally constitute the opposite of heights. The abyss is as far as possible from the zenith. Yet bodies of water reflect the sky and the sky may reflect waters, as in a mirage. Heaven and the high places (Air, Mountain) were so placed in the I Ching family as to contact the ground and the deep (Earth, Sea), suggesting continuity and relatedness of even those things that seem most opposed.

The teaching was that relative highs and lows are only illusory. Every position in the cosmic scheme is as important as every other position. Therefore, each elemental spirit or principle stands close to a transformation into its opposite.

Any water occupying a declivity, descending into the earth-womb, could be likened to the waters of birth. Seas occupied the greatest declivities.

Therefore, shore dwellers often sent their dead out to sea in the expectation of rebirth from the universal womb. This theory underlay the Viking funeral and other forms of boat burial.

Sea water plus fire from heaven (lightning) was sometimes supposed to be the source of life's essential fluid, blood. The warmth and redness of blood were attributed to the holy fire, while its salty taste was still that of the sea. Oriental sages said the god from above gave up his life when his fire was quenched in the deep, sacrificing himself so other beings could live by the infusion of his energy.

This early idea of divine fatherhood by self-sacrifice was related both to the image of a dying god giving his blood to humanity and to the ascetics' belief that sexual contact depleted stored-up male energy and transferred it to the female, who might then use it to create her offspring. Out of the latter theory arose the ubiquitous symbol of the devouring female Pit, attractive but dangerous to masculine spirit. Out of the former theory arose many myths of gods who fertilized the primal Deep, from Uranus the pre-Hellenic "Father Heaven" castrated and cast down to the abyss, to the great phallic World Serpent of Orphic creation myth, who also entered the lowest depths after giving up his creative energy to the primal Goddess of salt water.

Air
over
Sea

9. *Conduct, Treading Carefully* (Lu)

The opening of the second octave, ruled by the female Deep, indicates that even Father Heaven must tread carefully over her hidden abysses. Propriety and caution are indicated by the commentators' statement that this is like treading on the tiger's tail. A misstep will bring disaster.

The symbol of water open to the sky is deceptive. There may be thin ice or confusing reflections. The I Ching speaks of a half-blind man who falsely believes he can see clearly. One can mistake a reflection for the thing itself.

In regard to careful conduct to avoid mistakes, the I Ching makes its usual recommendation for dignified behavior and proper attention to traditional guidelines.

Sometimes the world was seen as a house of illusion, another meaning of the name of the Creatress, Maya, who entered Chinese tradition as Moye or Mo-he, the mother of Fu Hsi. Her technique of creation was magic, or illusion, an idea that led several Oriental philosophers to claim that the perceived world has no real existence. Her "house"—that is, the world—offered many choices, but like a magical house of mirrors, its appearances veiled their real nature or consequences.

In the house of mysteries over an unseen abyss, only one outcome shows plainly in the open air: death, represented by the ubiquitous figure of the hanged man between heaven and earth. A red carpet, emblem of the blood stream, seems to indicate a middle way, where fatal choices can be mostly avoided. Thus in the created world with its magic and illusion, careful conduct is always advisable in the presence of life's enigmas.

Sea
over
Sea

10. *Joy, Sea, Lake, Deeps* (Tui)

After proceeding with careful conduct, joy and pleasure are obtained by elimination of Air and duplication of Sea. Hindu sages equated duplication of waters with the idea of love, calling true love a process of merging as complete as the pouring of water into water. True love constitutes the truest joy. Thus, the Deep calling to the Deep was taken to symbolize merging of the inner selves, in loving exchange of cooperation, kindness, and fresh insight.

Twinning of the Youngest Daughter symbol also suggested a closeness like that of young girls whose friendship is unmarred by rivalry, so their trust in one another is boundless.

As the sight and sound of water has the ability to soothe the human spirit, whether it be a bubbling stream, a calm lake, a majestic river, or a churning surf, and as a drink of water satisfies bodily thirst, so the satisfaction and repose indicated by this hexagram were perceived as physical and spiritual at the same time.

Since this is a feminine octave, the symbol of joy is communion between female entities: a mortal woman peacefully contemplating her divine Mother Nature. Patriarchal societies tried to deny women such healing and refreshing communion with Nature, fearing the powers women might thereby develop. Romans even articulated this fear in a belief that the feminine power of water is dangerous to men.

Yet men have always felt attracted to the combination of water and femininity. Love, especially sexual love, was often compared to the properties of water. Therefore the Goddess as lover often personified the sea, as in Aphrodite, Isis, Marah, Mari, Themis, Thalassa, Tiamat, Pelagia, and various female water spirits: mermaids, naiads, nixies, wilis, sea fairies, sirens, and the ancient Fish sign meaning "woman."

Fire
over
Sea

11. *Estrangement,*
Opposition (K'uei)

Sages of the I Ching predicted good fortune in small matters here, to avoid the less agreeable assertion that things had gone wrong in larger matters. A death of love seems to have been indicated: not only lovers' quarrels *per se* but loss of harmony in almost any kind of relationship where emotional harmony is the primary essence of the connection.

Fire and water were said to be opposites that may attract each other, but their union would have to destroy one of them. Fire can boil water away. Water can quench fire. So the elemental family system of the I Ching anthropomorphized them as two sisters who couldn't agree, because their wills move in opposite directions. The fire strives upward. The water flows downward. Such personalities couldn't attain harmony except in brief, unusual circumstances, as when fire can live on water's surface in the form of burning oil.

Fire over the sea recalls the classic symbol of the fiery fertilizing god, as lightning descending like a lover into the female Abyss, which eats him up and extinguishes his spirit. However, new life was said to arise as a result of the male deity's self-sacrifice to the female. There was fear of the devouring female even though life could not go on without her, and such fear, too, could be a factor in estrangement.

Fire of the setting sun illuminates a reversed cross, in former times symbolic of the daily passage of the Father called Petra or Pater into the sea's womb for his rebirth. Such pagan traditions inspired the Christian legend of the immolation of Peter (Petra) on a reversed cross. Actually, the cross was an emblem of a male sacrificial god long before Christianity, and its reversal indicated the god's descent.

Water in the form of snow, the shroud of the dead year, covers the descending sun. Loss of harmony or wholeness is represented by the ruin of a sacred building, and the cold barrenness of a wintry scene, where only one single votary still half-remembers the ancient ways. Estrangement is sad, but continuing devotion even in the face of icy opposition may result in a resurgence of genuine feeling.

Thunder
over
Sea

12. Subordination, The Marriageable Maiden (Kuei Mei)

This hexagram's traditional interpretation of Marriageable Maiden seems at odds with its dire predictions: any action will be evil, any advance will bring misfortune, no goal is favorable, there is no advantage in doing anything. Or again, thunder over the Deep is said to signify man's end and man's beginning—that is, woman as a death symbol, preceding rebirth from the same devourer. The ancient Greeks said if a sick man dreams of marriage, he will die. Garlanded like a bridegroom (or a sacrifice), he must pass into the realm of Hecate as Mother Death and give himself up to her power.

Another interpretation of this "subordination" may have been addressed to the Maiden herself, warning of a death of her identity in marriage where she is not respected. Some said the maiden would marry only to become a concubine. This perhaps meant prostitution of a talent or misuse of one's early promise.

One already trapped in a subordinate position—that is, in the depths— was advised to be patient, refrain from confrontation or protest, do what is necessary, and develop inner vision for a better future.

Another interpretation cites fertility, for the thunder announced the entering of the lightning god into the waters of the Deep, so that the mating of male and female deities was accomplished and would bear fruit.

A triple sequence of subordination appears with the coming of a Night-Mare to haunt the man who enslaves a maiden. The Night-Mare form of Diana, Demeter, or Ceres was also "maiden"—that is, unmated—to maintain her power. One of her functions was to punish men who violated matriarchal law by depriving wives or concubines of their human rights. Therefore, she illustrated some of the paradoxes of human societies poised between older systems of mother-right and newer systems of father-right. For instance, if women had to remain aloof from marriage to retain their personal freedom, then how could men become fathers in order to exercise their newfound paternal rights? Or, if women were so obviously essential as the very foundation of the patriarchal society, how could they be entirely deprived of social power? The Night-Mare was one of the common symbols of deep-seated male insecurity even within the patriarchal system.

Breath
over
Sea

13. *Insight, Inner Truth, Sincerity* (Chung Fu)

Out of the coercive atmosphere of subordination, one may develop inner vision that will lead on to enlightenment. The sages stated that such insight can motivate even pigs and fish, creatures of the earth and the abyss respectively. An inferior position, therefore, can result in superior attainments of the intellect or the emotions. It can bring closer study of the motivations of others and a quicker instinct for predicting from small clues how they will behave. A person who has learned such lessons is in closer touch with the truth.

Breath or wind passing over the sea, stirring it, also recalls the basic creation myth of the universe born from an abyss stirred by the Goddess's word, song, or dance, or by the breeze of her passing. In such stirring of ther mind's unconscious abysses there is the possibility of emergence of new impulses of creativity and understanding.

In the ancient world, insight or inner vision was represented by the Kore (Maiden) in the Eye, that is, the tiny reflection of the self, seen in the pupil of another's eye. This phenomenon was also known as the baby, daughter, virgin, psyche, soul, or apple of the eye. As the apple of her Mother's eye, Kore the Maiden stood for the soul of the earth, which was Demeter, her Mother. Her sign, a five-pointed star, is still found in the core of every apple.

As the "in-sight" or soul in the eye, the gentle Kore-maiden might drift in the salt waters of the inner aqueous humor, the eye's inner sea, looking out of the rose window of the pupil upon the external world.

Water
over
Sea

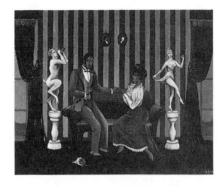

14. *Restraint, Limitation* (Chieh)

This hexagram counsels self-imposed limitations such as thrift, self-discipline, control of emotions. No matter how much talent is present, no art can reach its full flowering without discipline in training and using the natural gift. Lessons learned in the subordinate position of student or apprentice prove valuable later. Those who are not self-controlled must be restrained by outside influences.

Water, the element of the deeps, weighs down upon itself to generate internal pressure. Restraint may direct internal pressure to useful purpose, as water under pressure can flow through pipes to do productive work. Not even the seas contain all the essence of elemental Water. The incompressible substance is limited by what its beds or vessels can hold.

Though severe limitations may seem onerous, the basic rules of nature are never relaxed for any reason. Thus the world remains in good order. It is said that human beings should follow the natural law, to obtain maximum benefit from life.

There are also wrong types of limitation, restraint for its own sake, as a pointless exercise of power. This hexagram warns against such abuses of the natural need for limits.

The Western world knew one of its most hypocritical periods of social restraint in the eminently patriarchal nineteenth century. Elemental powers of sexuality and emotion were supposed to be under rigid control but were actually generating enormous internal pressures to be expressed in war, exploitation, and cruel psychic disorders. To account for their own suppressed urges toward a freer ethos (represented by their own romantic vision of antiquity's nymphs and satyrs), men evolved the stereotype of female emotionalism or unruliness. Thus, conventional men could react with horror to any woman's attempt to revive the free ideal of the classical era, which could really be admired only as an art form and not as a blueprint for living.

Mountain
over
Sea

15. *Decline, Loss, Reduction* (Sun)

Depths held in check by the weight of Mountain signify a decline of inner force. Though pressure may be excessive, yet it is a natural process and must be accepted by reduction in the number of matters to be dealt with.

This hexagram traditionally calls for simplification appropriate to an inevitable loss of resources. Any attempt to maintain earlier levels of power would be out of touch with reality. The sages say, if there is nothing else to offer to the divinities, two small vessels will be enough. Like the Gospel story of the widow's mite, such images of decline and loss meant that one should offer only what is within one's power and refrain from exhausting reduced assets by ill-considered ostentation. What diminishes the possessions of the lowly can only go to increase those of the exalted, who are not in need.

Sea under the mountain was a common mythic symbol of the Land of the Shades, or underworld, attainable by a boat trip on black nether waters of death and rebirth, which Greek mystics called the Styx. The Goddess Persephone, Queen of the Shades, was said to greet incoming souls at her white tree by the fountain of Lethe, "Forgetfulness," whose magic would make them forget their former lives. Orphics taught that one must not drink the water of Lethe if one wished to retain a whole memory and so find a desirable incarnation for one's next life. Greek heroes were depicted as exercising this choice in the underworld.

Not only Orphism but mystery cults in general taught the Oriental doctrine of reincarnation, with various ways to get past the gatekeepers and guardians of the afterlife, often by self-identification with a martyred savior, who had entered the realm of the dead and returned with a gift of enlightenment.

Earth
over
Sea

16. *Approach, Promotion* (Lin)

This hexagram represents a fresh approach to success and happiness. Progress is noted for those who have met inevitable decline with appropriate measures, behaving with proper modesty and caution. Earth over Sea is equated with the end of winter and the first beginning of spring, when new green shoots appear. Water rising up from under the ground was likened to sap rising in the vegetation, announcing a new season of plenty.

The present is said to be propitious, even if opportunity can't last forever. Some misfortune is proposed for the eighth month, perhaps indicating normal decline and decay associated with the waning of the year. A person in authority may arrive to inspect a situation. Prosperity comes closer, for those who can respond to new challenges.

One popular notion of approaching happiness in paradise was embodied in the survivals of Europe's pagan fairy faith, which taught that devotion to the Goddess (Fairy Queen) could win felicity in her land of eternal springtime. After behaving with proper modesty and deference toward feminine powers, an adept could be escorted across the blood river (or Styx) to this happy land.

Perhaps the Fairy Queen's most famous devotee was the medieval magician-poet Thomas Rhymer. His aptitude with word magic and spells was attributed to his seven-year stay in fairyland. Poems sometimes spoke of the goddess as Queen of Earth, approaching on high above the vitalizing waters that brought new life to all her lands, promoting fertility and every other kind of benefit.

6

The Third Octave (Li)

Fire is the element of the third octave, designated female in the I Ching, though most Oriental traditions identified fire, sun, and lightning with the male principle. However, like pagan Scandinavians, the Chinese and Japanese called the sun a Goddess. In Japan the Sun Goddess was viewed as the primal ancestress of the imperial clan.

Oriental philosophers admired the beauty of fire, as well as its day-to-day usefulness in cooking food or warming the body. Therefore the term for fire in the I Ching also means beauty. Yet it was not forgotten that fire must be handled with care and respect, for it can become vicious. The ancients naturally feared many ordinary manifestations of the uncontrolled fire principle: lightning, lava, brush fires, parching drought, or the internal "fires" of feverish illness, as well as household fires inadvertently set.

The element of fire was often zoomorphized as a lion or a lion-headed Goddess, beautiful but dangerous, capable of turning on those who tried to tame her. Egypt's Mother Hathor in her destroying aspect as the Sphinx offers a common example.

Some traditions indicate that fire represented knowledge of civilized skills in general and that stealing this knowledge from the jealous gods was humanity's true original sin. The actual theft was often attributed to a godlike hero, worshiped as a god in his own right and often shapeshifted into the guise of a bird to fly up to the solar heaven of elemental fires. This popular legend extends all the way from the Garuda bird of

50

southeastern Asia to the Promethean, and later Roman, eagle. Prometheus brought down fire from heaven against the will of Father Zeus. He gave this forbidden kowledge of fire to men, to help them better themselves. Having never intended that men should better themselves, the jealous Heavenly Father punished Prometheus with eternal torture—as he was also supposed to have punished Eden's serpent, who was called Lucifer the "Light-bringer," for similarly giving forbidden knowledge to humanity. The Eden serpent probably evolved from the Middle Eastern concept of lightning as a "fiery flying serpent." In the older mythologies as in the story of Eve, it was the Goddess who received his gift on behalf of humanity.

Sometimes the gifts of fire and civilized skills were given by the Goddess herself. In memory of such legends, perpetual fires burned on the altars of some of the oldest Goddess figures, such as Vesta in Rome and Brigit in Celtic Brigantia. Such fires were never allowed to go out, because they represented a burning spirit or soul of the whole land, just as a maternal hearth fire represented the living heart of every ancient clan.

Air
over
Fire

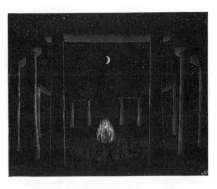

17. Fellowship, Community, Friends, Lovers, Union (T'ung Jen)

Fire open to the Air suggested a camp or the center of a ceremonial circle, symbolizing a place where like-minded persons could engage in communal activity. Fire warms each member of the group. The center is occupied by one beloved by all.

A sense of fellowship has long been associated with the identification of fire with the sun, when it was believed that both were the same element: "As above, so below." Groups are best unified by a bright vision like sunlight, shared among members. Common purpose draws individuals together for the benefit of all. In literal truth, this is the genesis of civilization: not individual genius, but group effort and cooperation, of which the focus on a central fire was an appropriate symbol. In ancient Rome, the word *focus* even meant fire on the hearth tended by the clan mother.

Universal throughout ancient Europe were many variants of the Latin word *nemeton*, an open-air temple in the form of a sacred grove or circle of standing stones. Such temples represented the immanent body of the Nature Goddess who had such names as Diana Nemetona. Within her charmed circles, her tribal children danced around sacred fires in ceremonies of union and communion. Like the clan matriarch herself, a central fire warmed and fed members of the group, drawing them together for light and protection. Sometimes, fire symbolized a group soul.

Sea
over
Fire

18. *Revolution, Uprising, Renovation* (Ko)

This hexagram suggests one purpose of the fellowship group: to unite in overthrowing an earlier order. Transformational change, as in a sudden revolution, is indicated. The process seems untrustworthy until after it has been accomplished.

Fire below the depths is like a submarine volcano, erupting despite great pressure from above, making violent changes in the environment. The term for this hexagram refers to a changing of skin or outer covering, as a volcano may alter the area around itself, changing fertile places to barren ones. There is mention of mutual destruction between two opposing forces, as inimical toward one another as fire and water. Only later, when the upheaval has settled down and has become subject to ordinary processes again, can the region find peace and confidently assimilate the changes that have been made.

Revolution is represented by a fiery leader rising up from the depths— that is, a volcanic ocean god like Poseidon or Dagon, combining the elements of fire and water. Like the old abyssal gods he is part man, part fish, carrying the trident that used to symbolize his union with the Triple Goddess and the "fire" of his ardor. Myths suggest that the abyssal gods used to covet earthly and heavenly kingdoms, and sometimes plotted to overthrow the heavenly Fathers whose rule, however tyrannical, could not extend to the lowest depths. That is why Christian fathers made their version of Lucifer a fiery dragon in the deeps—older myths had cast him in that role already. After all, to an incumbent autocrat, any rebel seems another Lucifer.

Fire
over
Fire

19. *Beauty, Fire, Intelligence* (Li)

Light and clarity are indicated by the duplication of Fire, suggesting a peaceful, productive period after a shake-up. Two tongues of flame arise, always a good omen, interestingly similar to the ancient symbol of Vesta: a double flame arising from an altar, taking the shape of two horns of the sacred cow. Strangely enough, Chinese commentators described this hexagram as two rearing cows representing good fortune.

Fire is traditionally identified with ardent energy, heat, passion, and enlightenment as well as beauty. The I Ching made fire a female power and refrained from mentioning her destructive potential. Perhaps the generally euphemistic approach of courtly interpreters forbade any hint of this, just as the ancient Furies were called "The Good Ones" to placate them and avert their wrath.

The hexagram of Fire implied not only brightness but also attachment, like the persistence of fire in clinging to its burning object and the difficulty of controlling its voracity. Similarly, real intelligence is hard to control when it seizes an idea and begins to develop new conclusions.

Fire was often associated with the beauty and clarity of crystals, because of the apparent power of a crystal to draw down "fire from heaven" like Prometheus and ignite tinder by focusing sunlight through its lens.

Fire "dances," so it was often represented by a dancing priestess, who also embodied beauty and intelligence as Goddess qualities. Such priestesses often used snakes in fire ceremonies, since snakes were symbols of wisdom and sacred to the Mother as her "fiery flying serpents."

1. *Heaven, Air, Sky, Authority*

2. *Resolution*

3. *Wealth, Great Possessions*

4. *Power, Greatness*

5. *Clouds, Small Nurture*

6. *Waiting, Calculated Inaction*

7. *Energy, Great Nurture*

8. *Peace*

9. Conduct, Treading Carefully

10. Joy, Sea, Lake, Deeps

11. Estrangement, Opposition

12. Subordination, The Marriageable Maiden

13. Insight, Inner Truth, Sincerity

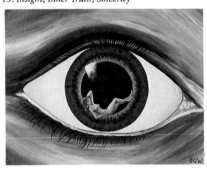

14. Restraint, Limitation

15. Decline, Loss, Reduction

16. Approach, Promotion

17. Fellowship, Community, Friends, Lovers, Union

18. Revolution, Uprising, Renovation

19. Beauty, Intelligence, Fire

20. Abundance, The Zenith

21. Family

22. Completion, Equilibrium

23. Elegance, Grace

24. Darkening, Injury, Repression

25. Innocence, The Unexpected

26. Following, Adaptation, Accord

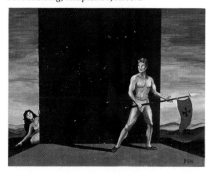

27. Gnawing, Reform

28. Shock, Thunder

29. Gain, Benefit

30. Difficulty

31. Nourishment, Mouths, Jaws

32. Return, Repeating

33. *Temptation, Contact, Sexual Meeting*

34. *Excess, Strain*

35. *Cauldron, Sacrificial Vessel*

36. *Endurance, Continuance*

37. *Gentleness, Breath, Wind, Spirit*

38. *Well, Source*

39. *Decay*

40. *Ascending, Advancement*

41. Conflict

42. Adversity, Oppression, Weariness

43. Incompletion, Before Ending

44. Release

45. Dispersal, Dissolution, Scattering

46. Abyss, Water, Danger

47. Immaturity, Ignorance, Inexperience

48. Army, Collective Force

49. Retreat, Withdrawal, Yielding

50. Attraction, Pleasure

51. Travel

52. Smallness, Details

53. Development, Progress, Partnership

54. Trouble, Obstacles, Difficulty

55. Stillness, Mountain, Solitude, Meditation

56. Modesty, Moderation

57. Stagnation, Standstill

58. Assembling, Gathering

59. Progress

60. Repose, Harmony

61. Contemplation

62. Unity, Joining, Coordination

63. Splitting, Peeling Off, Deterioration

64. Nature, Earth, Creation

Thunder
over
Fire

20. Abundance,
The Zenith (Feng)

Proper worship of the beautiful and exercise of intelligence lead to high achievement, fruitfulness, and plenty. Thunder above the fire was said to bring copious rain and lush fertility. Pregnancy and birth were indicated, either figuratively or literally.

This hexagram was taken as a zenith of attainment. Still, it must not be forgotten that the sun is enthroned at the zenith only for a moment, that the most brilliant light must begin to dim, and that every ascent is followed by decline. Thunder and lightning are awesome but last only for seconds. Human life is similarly ephemeral in the cosmic scheme.

Commentators say the magnificence cited by this hexagram is like the entrance to a very large house, which may be a metaphor for soaring to the heavens.

The fire spirit stands at a pinnacle, brandishing thunderbolts, which represent divine power but are also dangerous. Like lightning, glory is brilliant and also ephemeral. The heavy dark wings of the fire spirit may suggest effortful flight or forces drawing her downward from her high stance.

Breath
over
Fire

21. *Family* (Chia Jen)

As a logical development from the fruitfulness of the previous hexagram, this one refers to human fertility. There is fellowship around the unifying hearth in the seventeenth hexagram, but the air above is abstract, a heavenly atmosphere, rather than intimate human breath. By contrast, this is the circle of relatives closely involved with one another, living or having lived in the same area, breathing the same air, influencing one another's thoughts and actions.

Such a realm is sacred to women, who produce the family from their own substance and nurture living flesh from their own bodies. This fire is female and maternal, bringing individuals together, celebrating their relationships. The household and the feminine clan system stabilize the world. There is the suggestion of an "authoritative ruler" representing the matriarch whose breath blows the holy hearth fire.

However, later patriarchal commentators on this text urged the man of the house to establish "restrictive regulations" to forbid his wife and children to smile, laugh, or talk among themselves.

Naturally, such restrictions would have opposed the warm bonds between women and children of the household, catering to the Confucian "superior man" who could set them at odds with one another. Earlier, tightly woven matrilineal clans were the essential units of Chinese society, the same system as in the rest of Asia as well as in ancient Europe. Chinese family names are still based on a sign meaning "woman," a relic of past female control of the family. The blood bond passed down the generations from mother to daughter. Males were not directly connected to the bloodline, because they didn't form offspring out of their own inner blood. Their relationships necessarily passed through mothers and sisters. The true spirit of the clan was female even for a long time after the discovery of biological paternity, for "blood" relatives could come only from the maternal line. Women were thought to create their progeny from the magic blood given them by Mother Moon, whose festivals in ancient China could be attended by women and children only. The same ideas were extant in ancient Europe, which is why patriarchal systems were so anxious to masculinize family names, codify father-son relationships, and record male ancestry only, as in the biblical "begats." However, the primary idea of family is found in stair-step generations of women and their blood bond.

Water
Over
Fire

22. Completion, Equilibrium

(Chi Chi)

Water appears over the hearth fire, perhaps quenching it with a last communal cup. Something has come to an end. There is parting, either with or without regret. Opposing forces are evened out. Peace reigns for the moment, but adversity may come. Any movement away from equilibrium means disorder.

An ancient image of completed fertilization was the (female) water closing over the (male) lightning, whose fire animated sea water with the warmth and redness of living blood when quenched in the uterine deeps. Thus, a necessary sacrifice of the male principle to the female principle created the conditions for existence.

This kind of completion may be suggested by the message of this hexagram, which counsels patience and a calm anticipation of whatever the future may bring. To illustrate, a man and woman turn calmly away from an empty throne, whose abandoned robe of state and quenched candle indicate completion of the royal sacrifice. The figures complement one another, both robed in white, like priest and priestess. Whatever their joint functions may have been in the process just completed, they part with serene indifference, seeming secure in the knowledge that whatever had to be done was done, and now it is over.

Mountain
over
Fire

23. *Elegance,*
Grace (P'i)

Esthetic pleasures arise from harmony and balance. In the picture of this hexagram, the dark and stable bulk of the mountain is illuminated by fire at its foot, shining like stars in the night, a combination of what is motionless with what is always in motion.

Such an environment echoes the tranquilly balanced soul. Rooted in the warmth of affection, elegance flowers in creative expression, like a mountain ascending through brilliance to the heights of heaven.

This is an enriching and inspiring time when lovely things may be seen: a garden, silk garments, adornments, a white rider on a white steed. Because stars are the ornaments of heaven, one may contemplate stars to ascertain the correct seasons for one's actions.

The Western equivalent of the white rider on the white horse was Lady Godiva, whose name meant "Goddess" and whose naked ride through Coventry was once considered necessary for each season's renewal of every grace of nature. Without her influence, there could be no spring flowers, no return of the crops. Her silken adornment was her hair, which concealed her body, according to the popular legend. However, the whole point of the May ride of the White Goddess originally was not that she be concealed, for her divine nakedness was thought essential to general fertility.

Ecclesiastical authorities later forbade the people to witness Godiva's annual ride; hence the story that everyone (except Peeping Tom) refrained from watching her. Yet even after her pagan rites were extirpated, she still persisted, in the nursery rhyme, as the "fine lady on a white horse" that everyone went to see at the crossroads.

Earth ▂▂ ▂▂
over ▃▃▃▃
Fire ▃▃ ▃▃

24. *Darkening,*
Injury,
Repression (Ming I)

Light enters the earth and is extinguished. The sun sets. The Lord of Light is wounded and sinks down. That which was formerly sustaining and nourishing has failed. Elegance and esthetic refinement may slide over into decadence. A ruler becomes weak. Cruder, heavier forms threaten to overwhelm the beautiful.

This hexagram bore gloomy connotations, appropriate to the ending of the Fire octave, since the ending of any fire is to go out. Therefore, it meant the conclusion of a period of brilliance, comparable to the banking of a fire with earth.

The light is said to be veiled but not truly dead. The Lord has "entered the belly." The next day's rebirth of the solar hero was always expected. As a resurrected god, he would be greeted with the ritual phrase "He is risen." One who remained in the earth and failed to fulfill the usual role of the resurrected hero was said to become a ruler of the underworld among the dark elder gods.

There was a suggestion of a fiery cataclysmic ending to a more peaceful period, when all fires had seemed nicely tamed for the use of an enlightened, affluent civilization. Such doomsday visions occur in all mythologies, including our own. Some traditions held that the cataclysm would be brought on by the excessive greed and violence of men and their male gods, who forgot to honor the Goddess's laws, the principles of motherhood, and family loyalty, the foundations of life. Therefore, their own evil would destroy them.

As a result of this prophesied cataclysm, motherhood in the after-time could manifest itself only as a terrible accusation in the eyes of women clutching their dead children in a black, poisoned, starving land. The Madonna figure changes to a spirit of the Waste Land, which medieval seeresses described as all that would be left of the earth after the upheavals brought on by men's greed and rampant aggression. The Madonna figure was imagined as always merciful and forgiving, but the wronged mothers of the barren future, seeing their children dead, would never forgive.

7

The Fourth Octave (Chen)

This is the realm of Thunder, which can "put things in motion," according to the Chinese sages. Its association with the eldest son significantly recalls the perpetual conflicts between Heavenly Fathers and their Divine Sons, wherein the disputed rod of power, retributive weapon, phallic symbol, voice of authority, and general attention getter was the thunderbolt. Previous to the Christian image of the Divine Son abjectly obedient to the paternal will, other mythologies more overtly expressed basic Oedipal rivalry. Either the young god seized power to overthrow the elder one, or the Father successfully defended his commanding position and punished the hubris of his arrogant son with stentorian commands and destroying thunderbolts.

In Greek myth, Zeus the Thunderer voluntarily relinquished his power to the sacrificed son-savior Dionysus, but only after Dionysus had met the martyr's death that was ordained for him, according to the Orphic salvation cult. The demand that the son give himself up to death in order to obtain godhood was also typical of Christian theology.

Oriental symbolism represented the disputed royal thunderbolt as a double-ended scepter called *dorje* or *vajra*. It was understood to be a phallus, the "jewel" locked into the genital "lotus" of the Great Mother— the true object of all father-son rivalry. Often, like Maia, Mari, or Mary, she was both mother and spouse, for the theory of reincarnation allowed the god to be both father and son alternately, as one eternally destroyed the other and replaced him, and as all of nature was apparently recycled each year.

Humans often assumed the thunder was the fearsome, commanding Logos-voice of their highest god, whoever he was. The I Ching uses thunder as secondary element, communicating between heaven (Air) and earth: that is, whatever speech humans might hear from the lofty god. According to a clever Hindu story, later used by T. S. Eliot in *The Waste Land*, the thundering god spoke only one meaningless syllable, *Da*. All his hearers interpreted *Da* to suit their own individual beliefs, but the thunder went on mindlessly repeating only the same sound, "Da! Da! Da!"

It is perhaps significant that the old thunder gods were labeled devils by their Christian opponents, whereupon their combined form, *the* devil, became "Prince of the Power of the Air" and master of thunder and lightning. Yet, curiously enough, God also retained the power of the thunderstorm—which was known as an act of God—and so shared powers with the devil and presumably sent the lighting bolts that struck his own churches. Special prayers for protection against thunderstorms were actually so irrational as to invoke God against himself.

25. *Innocence, The Unexpected*
(Wu Wang)

This hexagram refers to a childlike state of innocence in which there is no thought of wrongdoing or cheating—the guilelessness of the young child before he senses the hidden Oedipal hostility of the elder male who rules over him and secretly fears his future strength.

Just as thunder may come suddenly from a sky that seemed clear or paternal wrath may catch the child completely off balance, so a sudden trouble may be brought on by thoughtless simplicity. Yet a surprise seeming at first disastrous, like a sudden illness or weakness, can prove beneficial in altering the outlook and actions to suit new circumstances. The unexpected can be an eye-opener.

Either by design or by chance, this hexagram occupies the same position in both King Wen's and Fu Hsi's systems. This may contribute to its interpretations of freedom from ambivalence or insincerity. It sometimes speaks of a person of incorruptible integrity, limpidly clear as blue heaven: this in itself unexpected by the cynical majority. Sages counsel avoidance of intrigue and advocate creative problem solving through spontaneous, guileless activity.

Female innocence was embodied in many fairy tales in the young girl who unexpectedly met a clever seeress or witch and became initiated into significantly feminine traditions that male authorities had tried to repress. Unless it was carefully concealed, such enlightenment would bring trouble. In her youthful enthusiasm for new learning, a girl might face unexpected danger because of her natural candor. However, when the opportunity to learn something suddenly presents itself, risks must be taken for the sake of enlightenment.

Sea
over
Thunder

26. *Following,*
Adaptation,
Accord (Sui)

This hexagram calls for sensitivity to the environment, both physical and social, and for flexible adaptation. Efforts to take control of a situation would be wasted. Even a leader must follow trends and adapt to the spirit of the times, or leadership will soon collapse.

The power of the thunderbolt is hidden in the depths of the sea, which means power must yield to environmental pressure. At times it is better to lie concealed, to adapt, to follow, even if one has the strength to lead. The greatest strength makes a willing beast of burden. Followers must obey, but rulers must sacrifice.

In context with adjacent hexagrams, this might refer to the son biding his time and saving his strength until the time comes to challenge the father.

Whether a following consists of one person or many, it may take on a life of its own that the leader never intended, like the ancient idea of a shadow that can become a separated soul. The formerly obedient following can threaten the leader with unforeseen dangers, becoming a nightmarish monster in its collective strength. At such times, a wise leader can only lower the banner and listen to the wisdom of others—perhaps especially of female others, whose intuition may see behind the scenes and understand the basic roots of both the leader and the threatening shadow.

Fire
over
Thunder

27. *Gnawing,*
Reform (Shih Ho)

A problem to be decided by legal process is like something gripped in gnawing jaws. The law chews slowly. A treasure or a talisman is buried in tough substance, which is being gnawed like dry meat on a bone.

Thunder and lightning here represent an obstruction bitten through, as a violent storm clears the tension in the air. Sometimes the biting appears to be more literal, as in deliberate mutilation of soft flesh to remove some physical part. Lightning, like a piercing knife, brings pain and complaint (thunder), but the end result is improvement. One recalls the classic myth of the father's castration.

Legal recourse is recommended where possible. The jaws must keep working patiently, as rainwater from recurrent storms can wear away rocks.

In the era of matriarchal law, the Triple Goddess as enforcer of the law was envisioned as a triad of Furies. Armed with sword, spear, and scourge, the Furies came down from fiery skies looking like black-winged, horse-tailed monsters who could chew flesh from bones with the fangs of their canine heads. Trying to flatter them and divert their anger, the Greeks called them Eumenides or Kindly Ones. Their strike was as feared as a bolt of lightning. Their attention was always attracted to the *miasma*, a scent of spiritual pollution that clung indelibly to any offender against the Mother's law. Certainly an attack by the Furies would have had the effect of bringing reform.

Thunder
over   ⚏
Thunder

28. Shock, Thunder (Chen)

As if that which was gnawed falls apart suddenly with a terrible noise, so there comes a frightening shock that may bring laughter, shouting, or screaming. There is uproar in the elements and in the mind. Terror stimulates surprising actions.

A son may seize power from the father under cover of disorder and chaos. It is said that when the time of movement comes, established authority will be filled with dread, like a tyrannical father guiltily fearing the vengeance of the maturing son. Despite his apprehension, he "yet smiles and talks cheerfully." Still, when his bluff is called, he sees great peril and may sink down to a position of weakness. By extension of this idea, the shock can mean abrupt, startling power shifts that will cause distress and difficult readjustment.

A conflict of dragons was a popular mythic symbol of power shifts, in both the East and the West. To witness such a conflict was supposed to induce helpless terror, like that of a child trapped in a scene of violence between adults.

In a typical legend, the wizard Merlin in his childhood witnessed a fearful underground battle between a red dragon (Vortigern) and a white dragon (Uther). As a result of this dread vision, Merlin was able to prophesy the future. No temple could stand on its foundations until the battle was resolved, because the very earth quaked with the creatures' violence. Mystic powers, like Merlin's, were sometimes said to arise from a shock or terrifying experience early in life.

Breath over Thunder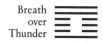

29. *Gain, Benefit* (I)

A gentle breeze, clearing away the thunderclouds, encourages the newly moistened earth to bring forth abundant fruits. Commentaries mention a plow, symbolizing a new season of fertility and nourishment.

From every activity there is profitable reward. It is a favorable period to undertake great works. Gifts from heaven soothe away the anxiety generated by former shocks, as a new incumbent in high office promises a new era of peace. When an objective is kept firmly in mind, progress can be made each day.

Influential people are enjoined to show generosity toward their supporters and to others on whose service they must depend. A new regime should not copy the mistakes of the old one. True benefit requires goodwill on the part of all.

The symbol of a begetting spirit was gentled in the medieval myth of the unicorn, who would come tamely to lay his (phallic) head in the lap of a maiden. Not only was he yet another version of the virgin-impregnating god, he also represented maleness mellowed by feminine influence and turned toward his rightful role, the fostering of fertility and abundance in a peaceful world. The unicorn stood for the ancient kings who were not allowed to rule unless they were married to the Goddess's representative, the Virgin of Spring, so as to bring forth a new season of benefit to all.

In Oriental imagery, thunder meant awakening, particularly the awakening of springtime, when early rains come, along with warm breezes to encourage new life. The Virgin and the Unicorn carried similar implications in medieval Europe.

Water
over
Thunder

30. Difficulty (Chun)

Heavy rains over thunder symbolize the storms of tribulation and trouble. New gains seem to come to a standstill, while the seeker's goals are temporarily lost to view.

The sages likened such difficulty to a traumatic birth attended by blood and pain. Something new is struggling to appear but seems blocked by adversity, disorder, and loss of control. Rain to nourish the future growth is brought by violent upheavals of heaven and earth. Sometimes, a reference is made to primitive earth conditions and the obscurity of primal chaos, from which later consolidation may draw success.

Early scriptures from the Middle East speak of the birth of the universe as a cataclysm comparable to the destructive upheavals of doomsday. Despite her huge power, the Mother herself suffered birth pangs. The Babylonians said she poured forth her blood for three years and three months in a massive stream to nourish all future life forms until the world's death. Mother Earth in travail was associated with such frightening phenomena as earthquakes and volcanic eruptions. Her fountain of blood was the Nether Upsurge, deliberately mistranslated in the Bible as a "mist" that went up from the ground.

Difficulty in an enormous task, like bringing a world to life, would be a correspondingly enormous difficulty. However, such Goddesslike efforts cannot be avoided, any more than the labor of birth can be avoided, if any true, stable existence is to be brought about.

Mountain
over
Thunder

31. Nourishment, Mouths, Jaws (I)

Nourishment of the world depends on fixed cycles of interdependence among life forms. It is important to observe closely, to determine what forms of nourishment—physical or spiritual—are required by the self and by others. Any type of nourishment must be applied at the right times and in acceptable ways.

Thunder in the mountain refers to melt-avalanches in early spring, which replenish the nourishing waters of the earth. Oriental symbolism usually equated mountains with the many breasts of the Earth Goddess whose fluid filled the mouths of all her children.

When such imagery is lost, there may be difficulties in relationships, due to lack of attention to proper nurture. One's own general sense of well-being depends on proper nurture of close associates, whose support will be needed. The sages counsel avoidance of greediness or excessive indulgence in feeding hungers.

The world-sustaining Goddess in mountainous form was enthroned on high amid her multitudinous children, among them the phallic Great Serpents sometimes represented by lightning: that is, the fiery flying serpents of the Old Testament or the lightning-descending Lucifer of the New. The ancient Goddess nurtured them and eventually chose one to become her consort and mountain-king. Even Zeus and Jehovah were shown as spirits of this type, in the first century B.C., when the mountainous Goddess was worshiped at Ephesus as Diana the Many-Breasted, giver of nourishment to the world's hungry mouths.

Earth
over
Thunder

32. *Return, Repeating* (Fu)

Appropriately placed at the midpoint of the Fu Hsi arrangement, "Return" signals the second half of the largest cycle, represented by the one solitary change in the whole arrangement of the bottom line, which changes from solid to broken between this hexagram and the next. Traditionally associated with this hexagram is a turnaround period of seven days. Since this is only one lunar quarter, not the megacycle suggested by the single change, commentators may have meant that seven days would be required for a proper reading.

Thunder within the earth suggests the ancient primal giants, whose movements were thought to cause earthquakes and bring back primitive conditions. They are mentioned in the Bible as the "giants in the earth" who lived before the Flood.

The I Ching's "Return" also meant a new beginning slated to unfold in due time, inevitably, without forcing or excessive energy. As spring follows winter at its own pace, so new developments must be allowed adequate time for their growth. Trying to hasten natural processes can only lead to ultimate frustration.

In the modern sense, giants thundering in the earth may be likened to the industrial civilization that gouges the mother planet with mines and tunnels, weighs her down with grimy concrete structures, kills her wildlife, and poisons her waters. As the climate of opinion began to turn against such manifestations of "progress," there arose some half-formed, half-understood yearnings for a return to gentler feminine images, as well as renewed reverence for the symbolic motherhood of the universe.

Thus, an idealized Queen of Heaven figure may rise behind the structures of contemporary life. Though she may stand silent, cool, still, and uncommunicative, yet she may draw the unspoken longings of men toward herself out of violent streets. Churches have tried to harness her power to their own ends, by mortalizing her and denying her a divinity that she actually commands in practice, but she is too vast an archetype to be contained in man-made religious systems.

In the I Ching, she symbolizes the single turning point in the largest of all cycles, known to the ancients as the still point of the turning worlds.

Only the return of the Goddess may counteract the ugliness wrought by centuries of concentrated patriarchy, which may be associated with the yang line underlying all other structures of the I Ching's first half. Henceforth, the underlying line is yin.

8

≡≡
≡≡
▬ ▬

The Fifth Octave (Sun)

Fifth in the continuum comes Breath, also called Wind, Breeze, Storm, Invisible Energy, and other manifestations of the Air element in conditions that are perceptible to human senses, as well as serving to maintain human life. Because the breath of the atmosphere was visible to the eye when it produced motion in the trees, the fifth octave was also associated with wood, which the Chinese sometimes regarded as a fifth element in itself.

Hindu sages called the soul of the world Atman or "breath," corresponding to the Greek *atmos*, air, and similar to the concept of *pneuma*, the vital spirit as breath. Pneuma was represented as a female deity, the Goddess Within. Most words for "soul" had a feminine gender everywhere in the world, deriving from primordial beliefs that all forms of indwelling vital spirit were female and mother-given, like the original "I-dea" or Inner-Goddess who was the source of all intelligence.

When men evolved the notion that a god's breath could be a begetter or creator, as in the patriarchal Logos theory, the indwelling spirit of intelligence was masculinized like the Roman *genius*, which originally meant "begetter" like its relative, the Arabic *djinni* or genie. This word also meant any man's soul. A woman's soul was a *juno*, named after the Goddess who was Queen of Heaven, hence of all the airs of heaven. Significantly, European culture chose to forget the word *juno* and adopt *genius* as the definition of intelligence.

Yet "inspiration" was literally breathing-in, and it was usually a female

72

figure like a Muse who gave this divine breath of creativity. She represented the air-soul from heaven, able to bring about possesssion by her spirit in the body of the "divinely inspired" poet, artist, or shaman. In the I Ching also, the holy spirit of Breath was female: like the first Muse, the eldest daughter of Mother Earth.

Air
over
Breath

33. *Temptation, Contact, Sexual Meeting* (Kou)

A new beginning is shown here by reversal of all the lines of the previous hexagram—the only point in the Fu Hsi arrangement where this happens. At this point, the first half of the system, founded on the yang line, meets the second half, founded on the yin line. Thus it is an appropriate expression for the place of contact between male and female principles.

Wind or breath designated female, moving under the heavens designated male, formed a symbol the Confucian philosophers considered proper for marriage. However, their insistence on correct subservience in a wife was constantly endangered by individual women not inclined to be subservient. Therefore the attraction of the female was secretly feared and labeled Temptation: man's perennial excuse for his own powerful desire for that which he wants to call undesirable.

Perceiving only weak women as comparatively harmless, patriarchal commentators interpreted the element of danger at this turning point (as all turning points were thought dangerous) as a strong woman. A man should not marry such a one, they said; yet the encounter seemed to be thought inevitable.

The combined image of father and eldest daughter in this hexagram recalls the numerous ancient eldest-daughter Goddesses who challeneged and defied their fathers, such as Anat, the elder Athene, Neith, Minerva, and Macha. Such warrior women were also present in the ancient mythologies of China. Their secular meaning seemed to be a powerful feminine spirit threatening to overthrow patriarchal authority.

Prepatriarchal imagery showed less fear of female powers. Ancient Egyptians didn't hesitate to personify all the starry sky as female: the Goddess Nut, or Neith, or Hathor, whose breasts produced the Milky Way. Her consort Geb lay flat on his back on the earth below, ever striving to reach her with an erect penis, symbolized by the obelisk. In this mythic conception, the high air meant Mother and the heated exhalations of the earth meant Father. Their contact was an energizing force that produced and sustained life.

Greeks inherited at least some of the concept, such as their belief that the star-milk of the heavens (*galaxios*) sprang from the breasts (*gala*) of Hera, Queen of Heaven. Formerly a universal Goddess of both heaven and earth, she was placed lower as her consort Zeus came to be raised up. So she began to personify the earth, while her Crone aspect, Hecate, ruled the underworld.

Sea
over
Breath

34. *Excess,*
Strain (Ta Kuo)

Temptation ineffectively handled produces an excessive weight of stressful factors, pushing a structure toward its breaking point. Temptation unwisely followed will cause strain, just as excessive eating strains the body with an overload of fat. A commentary said, significantly, that the lovers are too much together. The real, self-absorbed, untrammeled union of male and female was not an overtly admitted aim of the patriarchy.

Some sages equated the breath symbol with trees or tree roots, here buried under a weight of water, yet desperately attempting to put forth new shoots, to reach toward the free air.

To others, this hexagram denoted a bewildering confusion of too many ideas or considerations, symbolized by an overheavy roof causing the ridgepole to sag. Anything too large, too heavy, too much, or too exhausting may be represented by the breath oppressed under a weight like that of the sea. Those who dive too deep are hampered in movement and cannot breathe. It is said they bear the weight of the world on their shoulders.

Various gods were said to bear the weight of the world on their shoulders, including the Libyan-Ethiopian versions of Atlas-Prometheus, perhaps originally derived from the Egyptian earth god. The Atlas mountains were once his realm. Earthquakes were attributed to his convulsive movements under the massive burden of the earth. Some associated him with the old serpent-deity sent underground as a punishment; others prayed to him as a supreme god, hoping he would go on bearing the heavy weight, so life on earth could continue. Great burdens may also be great responsibilities.

Fire
over
Breath

35. *Cauldron,* *Sacrificial* *Vessel* (Ting)

This hexagram refers to the fire heating a cauldron when fueled from below with wood and wind, or breath. The Cauldron was a worldwide symbol of rebirth after dissolution. Many classic Goddess figures restored sacrificial victims to life after their sojourn in the uterine Cauldron. Demeter, Medea, and Cerridwen present well-known examples.

The Chinese also regarded the Cauldron as a womb symbol and a natural attribute of the Goddess. From the Cauldron came potions, inspiration, wisdom, and renewal. It was said to have "rings of jade" at the top, a reference to the nested spheres of heaven. Some ancient traditions described all the ascending heavens together as the Mother's azure bowl or cauldron overturned above the earth, corresponding to the seven black cauldrons below, in the underworld. Thus the whole universe dwelt within a series of vast uterine vessels, often equated with the body of the Goddess herself.

The Cauldron hexagram sometimes referred to renewal or sharpening of the senses, the logical accompaniment of magical or literal rebirth, hence of any ritual believed to renew youthful vigor after a period of chaos and trouble.

Cooking in the cauldron came to be regarded as an evil process of destruction, after patriarchal thinkers began to deny its power of rebirth and to equate it with witchcraft. However, certain myths show that dissolution in the goddess's cauldron was once thought a short route to the attainment of godhood. Even certain Roman emperors claimed to be "deified in the Cauldron." Medea, whose specialty was "medicine" made in her cauldron and named after her, was not really so evil as the Hellenes pretended. She was in fact the reincarnative Mother Goddess of the Medes.

Thunder ≡≡ ≡≡
over ≡≡≡≡≡
Breath ≡≡≡≡≡

36. *Endurance, Continuance* (Heng)

From the sacred cauldron rises a new self, perhaps an alter ego. This hexagram implies constancy, unflagging patience, and steadfastness in the line of duty. Despite adversity, the faith will be kept with rocklike, four-square endurance.

Thunder and wind (breath of heaven) are natural partners in the life-giving rain. This partnership seems to have been equated with the enduring qualities of a long, fruitful marriage. The sages said when the motive power is spent, it will begin again, like the buildup of natural forces toward more rain and of human parentage and desire toward new fertility.

A gigantic image of the androgyne, set in stone against the eternal sea, indicates the necessary and enduring partnership of all two-sexed life forms. Such male-female images were common in antiquity, even in medieval texts on alchemy and magic. Janus, the two-faced god of Rome, was originally an androgynous Janus-Juno. Hermes-Aphrodite and Adam-Eve were other versions. In the East, the androgyne was sometimes called the self-fertilizing creator, origin of all things: Kali-Shakti on the left or female side, Shiva on the right or male side.

Understanding is to be gained from study of all things whose natural tendency is to make solid, enduring joins and to continue throughout the ages. Inner truths are tested by time. A human being may comprehend truth only by contemplating that which lasts longer than humanity.

Breath
over
Breath

37. *Gentleness, Breath, Wind, Spirit* (Sun)

Gently penetrating breezes bring the breath of life to nature in each season of renewal. In its refreshing, nondestructive aspects, wind melts winter ice, carries the pollen, and stirs new growth.

Earth's creatures make contact with the Air element by way of winds, breezes, and their own breath, which gently enters living bodies from the surrounding air, then returns outward again to mingle with the air anew. The sages viewed this as an example of that which is constant though ever-changing. As air penetrates live tissues in the breath, so the eternal verities gently penetrate the mind that breathes them in as "inspiration." This should occur without strain.

Doubling of the Breath symbol also indicates certain words that should be repeated twice. Witch charms used to have this feature.

According to the pagan lore of Europe, the three sisters of Fate, Wyrd, or the "Weird Sisters" used to whisper secret charms of growth and renewal to the woods early in the spring. Sometimes, they could be glimpsed among the trees at night. Such a sighting was usually feared. The superstitious claimed that to see the Sisters about their work was to intrude on a holy mystery, which could bring dire results.

The symbol of breath in the I Ching could also mean wood, since the trees were considered media for perceiving the world's breath in branches stirred by the wind. Similarly, the Weird Sisters were associated with trees and sacred groves, like druidesses or dryads. Their ghostly presence was supposed to guard nature's holy places, where men might trespass only at their peril.

Water
over
Breath

38. Well,

Source (Ching)

As the thirty-seventh hexagram suggests the constancy of essential air, so the thirty-eighth suggests the constancy of essential water. It is said that dwellings can be moved, whole cities can be moved, but the well supplying water for the population can't be moved. The source must remain in its own place. Those who seek it must go there.

Here the symbol of breath is closely associated with its alternate interpretation, wood, indicated by the breath of heaven made visible through the movement of trees. The well is shown by water over the wooden vessel (bucket), which dips deeply to bring vital nourishment to the community.

A holy well is like the fount of wisdom: seldom greatly augmented, nor depleted, but constant. Its waters are serenely cool, like the intellect removed from passion. Once experienced, emotions should be put in proper context, understood, and calmly used for the sake of enlightenment. The Well symbolizes cool, dispassionate comprehension.

The Well appears in a serene setting, enclosed in a simple portico, whose slender columns and foliage-covered roof suggest the sacred grove. A woman carries the water above her own breath-of-life (that is, on her shoulder). Women traditionally represented the Source and the waters of life, as well as the essential connection between humanity and the revelations of nature. The woman who goes to the immovable source for her enlightenment is able later to carry the waters of life to others.

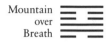

Mountain
over
Breath

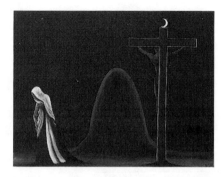

39. *Decay* (Ku)

As Breath, symbol of life, is buried beneath the mountain, there is an image like that of the savior god entering the dark earth and experiencing the decay of the flesh like mortals. This hexagram was persistently associated with a period of three days, the traditional dark-of-moon period of decay in the tomb for nearly every resurrected savior figure, East or West. Following the sacred knowledge implied by the preceding hexagram, this sounds very like the standard revelation of a mystery cult.

Since Oriental philosophies postulated rebirth following decay, a state of dissolution might be hailed as the first step toward reascending fortunes. Shamans used to believe their own powers dependent on a spiritual journey into death, decay, and refleshing. Crossing the Great River, another Chinese symbol of death, was also associated with this hexagram. On the other side, one would meet the blessed ancestors. The mistakes of ancestors must be set right, to help both them and their descendants achieve a peaceful afterlife. A savior could accomplish this.

With the rebirth of the new moon, after the three-day danger period known as the "ides" in Rome, the savior was resurrected and welcomed into heaven as a god. One element usually omitted from patriarchal versions of the myth was the essential femininity of the underground tomb-womb, whose gate was a yoni. The hero's death was traditionally viewed as a *Liebestod* or love-death, a sacred marriage, in which he voluntarily gave himself up to the powers of decay represented by the Goddess's Crone phase.

Rending the Veil of the Temple, as in the Gospel story, used to mean defloration of the Goddess's virgin or bride phase; the veil was called *hymen*. Thus, even early Christian fathers sometimes referred to Christ's cross as a "marriage bed." All three versions of the Goddess were present at the occasion, in the form of three Marys (the Moerae). The last of these would have taken the role of Crone-priestess and pronounced the death curse, Maranatha, on the holy bridegroom (1 Cor. 13:22). Since no one could survive the Crone-mother's curse, not even a god, his executioners would have been held guiltless on the ground that he was already doomed. Besides, he would rise again from decay, just as the new vegetation arose each year from the decay of the old.

Earth ▬▬ ▬ ▬
over ▬▬▬▬▬
Breath ▬▬▬▬▬

40. Ascending, Advancement

(Sheng)

After three days in the underworld, a culture hero of the Redeemer type would begin an ascent back to heaven, often through another rebirth from Mother Earth. One meaning of the fortieth hexagram, last of the Breath octave, shows a paternal Logos in contact with earthly Mater/matter: as Western scriptures would have it, "the Word made flesh."

Rising from the earth, breathing the air, being the air, the hero revealed "the Way" to his followers. Ascent of the breath principle was sometimes associated with its concomitant fifth element (in Chinese tradition), wood. Its upward thrust was likened to a springtime tree, rooted in the deep earth and rising toward heaven. Many sacred trees were connected with the resurrected savior figure, from the Dianic "King of the Wood" to the Christian image of the Rood. As a symbol of resurrection, the Christmas tree came not only from northern tradition but also from the pine tree of Attis, carried into the Mother's cave/womb as a decorated tree/phallus, so the god could beget himself again and be born again through the same Mother of Gods. Similarly, Osiris was a Redeemer resurrected from a tree, hailed as the god with a long member, "He Who Impregnates His Mother," the fulfillment of the Oedipal dream. Magical begetting or rebegetting could be brought about by the words revealed by the god to his priesthood, another interpretation of "the Word made flesh."

Wood was utilized also in the image of the Ladder of the Gods, whereby kings, pharoahs, shamans, prophets, and other privileged persons might ascend to heaven and become united with their deities. The ritual could include actual climbing of a tree.

Ascent means improvement of position in any aspect of life, a new vantage point, a better chance. It was said that when the Ladder of the Gods is presented, in any form, one should ascend without hesitation.

≡ ≡

9

The Sixth Octave (K'an)

Water was usually considered a feminine element, along with Earth. However, the I Ching made Water a son of the Earth, reversing the gender as also in the case of Fire, presented as a daughter of the Air.

As Fire represented the sun in the oldest mythic dualisms, so Water represented the moon. Ancient religions often regarded the Moon Goddess as the source of all waters, hence of all life, since fluid was the life essence for all creatures.

The moon provided the mysterious, sacred blood from which all women created their children *in utero*. Therefore, the Great Mother's inner blood was similarly credited with the original power of creation, as the Red Sea or Ocean of Blood from which matter first arose in the beginning. The ancients reasoned that the clotting process was initiated by the Goddess's churning motion, just as butter was clotted from churning milk. To some extent these anthropomorphic ideas were based on direct observation, since the moon did in fact cause the tidal churning of the seas. All observances were linked to the female principle in an era when reproduction was viewed as a female function only.

Early Greek philosophers said water was the *arché* or Mother-element, from which the other elements took their being. Noting that nothing could live without water, they regarded water as the essence of creation. With its savor of blood and its churning motion, the sea was traditionally equated with the primal womb and bore the common names of the Great Goddess, such as Maria, Marina, Marah, Mari-Anna, Mare, Mar, or

Mary. Even in her Christian disguise, she continued to wear the blue robe and pearl necklace of the ancient sea mother, who gave birth to the "risen" Light of the World (sun).

Water was often a symbol of love. In India and Egypt, vessels of water stood for deities in their sexual merging "like the pouring of water into water." The giving of a drink was considered an act of love, like a mother's giving of milk to her child. This symbolism explains the many mythological wells, springs, and holy fountains attended by women or female spirits, even in the Bible. The idea that the merciful Goddess gave certain waters for healing human ills passed directly into Christian tradition. Some of the same healing wells formerly sacred to the Goddess were simply transferred to Mary—usually via one of her miraculous appearances—and the pilgrimages continued undisturbed. From ancient female "waters" arose the rebirth ritual of baptism.

Water symbolized love as a graphic metaphor. It was said that like water, love would remain still and at peace in the open hand that held it gently, but it would disappear from the fist that tried to clutch and imprison it.

Because of its close association with the feminine principle, water was often used for divination. Mystics claimed to see insightful or prophetic reflections in a fountain or basin of clear water. In antiquity, images in water were often called external souls. To stir water that would break up a person's reflection was thought damaging to the soul. Here is the original rationale for the broken-mirror "bad luck" superstition still extant today. This also explains the I Ching symbol of water, a reflected broken line above and below the solid line representing surface, or an interface between two worlds. Sometimes the spirit world was imagined as an upside-down image of the earthly one. Female spirits that dwelt below the water surface (naiads, mermaids, wilis, and so on) were feared as ghost-women who could drag men down into their mysterious deeps.

Air
over
Water

41. Conflict (Sung)

Air and water combine and compete to make a storm, which churns the waters with high winds and fills the wind with driving rain. Such conflict of elements seeking to invade one another's realms symbolizes conflict between nations, persons, or family members. It could even symbolize inner conflicts between oppositional portions of the self. The discord could become very injurious. Obstacles arise in every direction.

The sages said that honor from strife really brings little credit to the combatant, even though popular ignorance declares the successful fighter heroic. Dissension divides and alienates those who should work together. No one can win such a conflict. The subject of controversy should be put aside and ignored for the sake of peace. Competitors were advised to avoid disagreements by an act of will.

Despite such advice, men retained their favorite legends of the great fighter or dragon-slaying hero, forced to earn his mysterious bride by facing extreme danger in an unequal conflict with a monster. Psychologists opine that the latter stood for the threatening father, trying to repress or destroy the son's sexuality. Dragon or giant serpent symbolized the larger phallus. The patriarchs more or less consistently confused fighting spirit with sexual prowess, believing that a display of one must prove the other, never noticing that a man who devoted his life to aggression was often ignorant of how to please a woman. Thus the world would be plagued by conflicts as long as men concealed the real meanings of sexuality from themselves and each other.

The woman, Goddess, Virgin, or princess-bride, awaiting the outcome of the conflict, was really the hidden essence of the hero's story. She was the goal necessitating confrontation with the dragon. It was seldom understood that, like the Bluebird of Happiness in one's own backyard, she could be won quite easily by men who came humbly and directly to her. For those capable of realizing the uselessness of the show of arrogance, conflict could be bypassed altogether. The stories and the shows were calculated to impress and scare away male rivals; they were performances for men, by men. Women's own choices could have been made without battles.

Sea
over   ☷
Water

42. Adversity, Oppression, Weariness (K'un)

One of the interpretations of this hexagram is a sinking into the dark essence of chaos for a period as long as three years, encountering bad times and misfortunte. True words may be spoken, but they will not be heard or believed. Circumstances are of the nature of deep waters: heavy, dark, cold, oppressive, and hostile to human life.

The sea or lake is viewed as having been drained into a deeper chasm, as if the primal Water element took back its medium of communication with the human world. Consequently, conditions revert to what medieval Europe called the Waste Land, a realm without creativity or comfort, subject to mindless hostility, inanition, and exhaustion.

When such adversity comes, one can only sink down with it and wait patiently for a time of change or relief. Sometimes, such adversity is taken as a test of character that prepares the individual to withstand greater trials in future.

Omens of oncoming adversity were thought to arise, in ancient times, from the chasms over which the sybils and pythonesses sat in their oracular caves. Inspiration ("breathing-in") came up from the deeps to the holy women who then prophesized the doom to come, for good or ill. When the feminine spirit of prophecy was suppressed by patriarchal religions, it might be said to have drained back into the deeps from which it came. The patriarchs closed the oracular shrines and called the seeresses insane.

Thus the intuitive powers of women were depleted, at a time when they were especially needed to foresee the moral evils that a male-dominated society would bring, to the greater oppression of both sexes.

43. Incompletion, Before Ending
(Wei Chi)

According to the King Wen arrangement, this hexagram comes last, in the number 64 slot, yet it is mysteriously labeled Before Ending. There is an implication of finality about this combination of elements, though the reading suggests something unfinished. Whatever is incomplete may have to remain so, when circumstances take away the possibility of further development. A sudden event may strike like lightning and stop something short while it is still in an incomplete state.

Some light may be shed on this inscrutable nomenclature by the worldwide myths of creation and doomsday characterized by fire and water: the Great Flood at the beginning of each successive universe, quenching and merging with the apocalyptic fires that end each preceding one. Of course, doomsday was always supposed to come without warning, like death itself, for which few individuals are ever really ready.

Apocalyptic fires came from the Goddess in her Destroyer aspect, according to the early myths that attributed doomsday to her curse on the incumbent gods for their selfishness and violence. As Kali, she devoured them all and burned up their world. Even in northern Europe, as Skadi the "Shadow," or Queen of the Shades, she did the same, sending her black wolf Fenrir to eat the sun. Her consuming of the gods was referred to as their Götterdämmerung, or Going-into-the-Shadow. Some Germanic myths connected her with Kali as a queen of fire from "the hot lands in the south."

Even the Gospels copied earlier authorities in insisting that doomsday, like death or any other catastrophe, would take nearly everyone by surprise. Life and work would be left incomplete. In the upheavals of the last days, there would be no more time for growth or building. Like a sudden lightning stroke, any disaster may similarly take away the possibility of further development.

Thunder
over
Water

44. *Release* (Hsieh)

Thunder and rain show in this hexagram, indicating active release of tension, as a thunderstorm violently releases built-up tensions in the atmosphere. The process of liberation may be stressful or destructive, but it brings relief and calm like the aftermath of a storm.

Sometimes, it is important to move ahead actively in the face of danger to achieve ultimate release. The hexagram counsels courage and steadfast refusal to be immobilized by stormy threats. Here, water is a danger sign and thunder means movement (away from danger), pointing to an escape. That which threatens must be actively challenged.

A witch releases herself from captivity by magical gestures and by the power of her rage. Her jailer, or would-be assailant, places enough credence in her powers to be intimidated. It often happens that doors open for those who are bold. Courage, a firm stand, and a show of fighting spirit may succeed, even for those who have been deprived of real power by adverse circumstances.

Breath
over
Water

45. *Dispersal, Dissolution, Scattering* (Huan)

As breezes dry up moisture and wind scatters the waves, so this breath-over-water hexagram represents a dispersal of forces and a disappearance of what was formerly plain to see, in the same way that water droplets disappear into the moving air.

Dispersal implies reunion at a later time, since every event was supposed to be followed by an equal and opposite reaction in due course. Breaking up is necessary, so a future reunion can take place in a different context.

Viewing the breath symbol as its sometime alternative, the tree or wood, some sages envisioned wooden ships departing for distant places. Others mentioned the sacramental scattering of sweat or blood in order to keep evil influences at a distance. Some kind of libation was implied.

Dispersal or dissolution of the dead used to mean a sea voyage to the western land beneath the sunset. Worthy folk—such as kings—were carried in special fairy ships attended by the Three Sisters in person, as in the legend of King Arthur. The boat would be wafted like a breath over the water, toward an eventual meeting with the Goddess herself in the realm of faery. All barriers would open, all mysteries would be resolved; the blessed dead would be given understanding of all things.

Egyptian pharaohs also anticipated perfect enlightenment in the paradise of Osiris, far away over the western sea. Souls would ride the outgoing tide and pass like a sea wind across the waters. Deceased ancestors were referred to as Westerners. It may have been the very idea of seeking the place of blessed souls that sent the first migrants from the Far East to colonize new lands in the West.

Water
over
Water

46. Abyss, Water, Danger (K'an)

This hexagram suggests danger: a shifting, fluid environment where nothing is sure or secure. Alien enemies may lurk in surrounding darkness, like creatures of the sea bottom.

According to ancient mythologies, water was the feminine element most dangerous to man, the swallower and quencher of his fire. As all life arose from the watery abyss as the primordial birth element, so all life would return to be swallowed up at doomsday. Thus, water symbolized the Mother as both creator and destroyer.

Water also meant the moon and her Crone form, the old moon as Mother Death, who was equally a figure of doomsday. Her "Deep" was her cauldron, to which all things must yield in dissolution, as suggested by the previous hexagram.

Fearing the shifty unpredictability of sea storms and flood waters, yet knowing the necessity of water to all forms of life, men assumed an attitude of cautious ambivalence toward this symbol. I Ching commentators mention water in a dangerous defile or cavern, common metaphors for female genitals, in connection with this hexagram of essential waters. A dark well in a secret place underground also hints at male sexual fears.

Sometimes, men seemed to believe an avenging female spirit of unsurpassed awfulness could rise from such an abyss, to threaten unwary males. She may have represented hidden guilts of the patriarchal system.

"Deeps" also meant the fear typically attending any prospect of immersion in the depths of the unconscious, the real repository of mythical monsters, which personified dark emotions long since judged unacceptable and suppressed.

Mountain
over
Water

47. *Immaturity, Ignorance, Inexperience*
(Meng)

According to the usual cyclic nature of Oriental symbols, dangers and dooms were followed by new growth, a new phase of immaturity, novitiate, or initiation, a childlike state renewed. Just as death could be followed by resurrection and rebirth, so the symbolic death—plunging into the abyss—would be followed by emergence in a washed-clean condition needing new enlightenment.

Immaturity was here equated with one who must seek out a teacher and pay careful attention to the teaching, so as not to ask the same questions more than once. Those who are ignorant should humbly seek instruction, being aware of their own ignorance so as not to give the teacher cause for impatience.

A mountain of lore was envisioned looming above the stream, luring the newly fledged one on to its great heights, attracting aspiration. But with treacherous, slippery footing, the aspirant may fall before acquiring enough wisdom even to get started on the climb.

A classic tale of warning against youthful ignorance was that of the young man Actaeon, who spied on the Goddess bathing in her secret pool under the mountain. He was turned into a stag, hunted down, and killed. The story descended from primitive sacrifices of the stag-king after his privileged view of the naked Goddess, and perhaps a sacred marriage with her. Ancestors, depicted as part of the mountain, bore witness to the event and passed on the warning: the unprepared or unenlightened should not trespass on mysteries they cannot understand. Actaeon's story suggested that to approach the essence of woman, man must be taught the right moves and the right attitudes of respect.

Earth
over
Water

48. *Army, Collective Force* (Shih)

Water, which usually stands for peace, is engulfed and hidden in the earth, leaving barren ground, in this hexagram of war. The underground water was sometimes taken to represent an undifferentiated collection of people moving together in the natural direction of the flow underneath them.

The leader gathers a great host of followers, inspiring them with his power. They look up to him as to an enormous idol, larger than life. Discipline takes control of the ignorance represented by the preceding hexagram, welding the unlearned masses into a formidable entity trained to conquer, as if the body of their chieftain grows gigantic and acts as a collective unit with a single mind.

The army is built up by discipline, which is the only way it can avoid corruption. If the army is corrupted by ignoble leaders, its spirit may become like a wild beast in the field or like one of the demon-gods of insatiable appetite. A war leader can become the sum of his destructive forces and take on demonic qualities, like a Hitler or a Frankenstein monster, grown huge by absorbing other lives. Commentaries mention wagonloads of corpses being carried away to be consumed, accompanied by mourning.

At the end of the Water octave, which began with conflict, the water has disappeared and removed its blessings of peace, comfort, and fertility. The army rules by, and is ruled by, fear. Still, the water remains deep within the earth and may be found again in another place and time. The collective power of armies is temporary by its very nature.

10

The Seventh Octave (Ken)

The Mountain represented an extension of the Earth principle into the realm of Air, as a real mountain could form a stairway to the clouds of heaven, however difficult or dangerous the ascent might be. High mountains were often regarded as the heavens in fact, known everywhere as dwelling places of the gods. Mountains were also places of mystic contemplation. A person who wished to commune with the world soul in holy solitude traditionally took up his or her position on a mountain.

The Goddess handed down her tablets of law to priest-kings at high altitudes on holy mountains, such as Mt. Dicte in Crete where she gave her commandments to King Minos. This custom was copied by later patriarchal gods, including the Hebraic Yahweh. According to the Sumerians, the Mother-Creator of the universe was the Mountain-goddess Ninhursag, whose name is still repeated as "a very holy word" by certain tribes in southern India. Ancient Phrygians called her Cybele or Ida. Early Greeks called her Gaea, Olympia, or Panorama, the "Universal Mountain Mother" who sustained all the later gods on her lofty lap.

Mountains were often envisioned as the many nourishing breasts of Mother Earth, producing the sources of rivers as sacred media of communion between her children and her essential spirit, likened to the communion between a human mother and her suckling. The milky-looking glacial streams common to high altitudes probably contributed a practical basis for such images of the "Many-Breasted" Goddess.

The effort of climbing a mountain was usually viewed as an initiatory

93

ordeal or a holy pilgrimage, to be rewarded with enlightenment. Perhaps this has something to do with the I Ching's placement of the Mountain octave just before that of Earth, the universal Great Mother, whose image forms the final revelation of the series just as the same naked World Goddess appears on the "last trump" of the Tarot cards' trump suit, the Greater Secrets. In the ancient East, nearly every mountain was thought to be the seat of a deity. The highest of them all, now known as Everest, was originally named Goddess Mother of the World.

So revered were holy mountains that people who settled in flat lands like Babylon and Egypt felt impelled to build artificial mountains as their holy places and tomb-shrines. Hence their ziggurats and pyramids. The original Tower of Babel was a ziggurat, Ba-Bel or "Gate of Divinity," forming the point of communication between heaven and earth. At its summit, the Goddess mated with the god-king.

Sometimes the holy mountain was called a bridge, a ladder, a route of souls to heaven, or a god's throne. The earth's high places always inspired awe. One way or another, they were always utilized as nature's greatest temples, where mortals and immortals could make contact.

Air
over
Mountain

49. *Retreat, Withdrawal, Yielding* (Tun)

As each octave begins with a problem to be solved, this one begins with the retreat of the mighty forces previously suggested. No matter how invincible an army seems to be, there is always a superior force that can make it retreat.

Similarly, any strength can meet its match and be compelled to yield, just as the strongest wind must yield when it meets the mountain. Thus, the sages said, it is unwise to put all of one's confidence in physical force alone.

This hexagram advises one not to try to compete with superior powers but to fall back and concentrate on small internal reinforcements. One must retreat "in a noble way," saving face. Encountering this apparently ignominious bit of advice, Confucian court seers insisted that it really meant "successful progress," like nearly every other hexagram they interpreted to please a ruler. Such self-contradiction is one of the major signs of the secondhand nature of the courtly canon, pointing to an older, underlying tradition that was more direct and did not try to express two opposite ideas at once.

To simpler minds, any encroachment on formerly sacrosanct areas was attended by superstititious fear of reprisal from powers mightier than any human effort. Retreat could be forced by any personification of this fear. For example, men bold enough to venture into areas formerly sacred to older, latterly discredited deities were thought to meet those deities in some demonic form. What happened next was the subject of many legends fearfully whispered around campfires in desolate places.

Seasonal times of retreat and withdrawal—like oncoming winter— were always under the jurisdiction of the Goddess as Crone, the death-dealer. Therefore, places formerly sacred to her were thought especially dangerous in the declining season, as at Halloween (Samhain, the feast of the pagan dead).

Sea
over
Mountain

50. *Attraction,*
Pleasure (Hsien)

This hexagram speaks of sea waves flinging themselves toward the rocky headland, which seems to resist their onslaught, yet imperceptibly breaks up little by little and falls into the water. Each is irresistibly drawn to the other. Thus after a strategic retreat, there may be another advance under inescapable compulsion, like the advance of the tides driven by the moon.

Sexual attraction and pleasure, love relationships, and marriage are hinted, with their usual implications of inevitability, their ups and downs, their promise of happiness exerting a powerful magnetism even if its fulfillment should be elusive.

A lake lifted high on the flank of a mountain is another image that implies a marriage of mutual assistance and nurture. Waters of the lake nourish the soil of the mountain, while the mountain collects clouds and snows to feed the lake.

Mountain lakes used to be avoided at night by men who used to believe the waters were inhabited by female spirits, whose fatal attraction would draw their victims down into the depths to drown. Various classical names for such spirits included naiads, nereids, nixies, vilas, or wilis. They were said to be the color of water or of moonlight, irresistibly beautiful as they danced or sat on the rocks combing their long hair. Like water wearing away stone, they could wear away the most determined resistance with their promises of unearthly delights.

They were, of course, symbolic of men's hidden fears of women's sexual attraction. Patriarchal authorities bent on destroying the pleasure bonds between the sexes evolved many different kinds of enticing she-demons and encouraged belief in their literal existence.

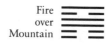

51. *Travel* (Lu)

Fire over the mountain is the allure of distant places. Sunset beckons the traveler ever westward to the promised land, just as Aryan tribes in the distant past colonized all of western Europe by following the sun, moon, and stars from the plains of central Asia all the way to the western edges of the continent. Even then, they imagined the lands of the gods even farther west, in sacred isles of the sea, where the sun still sets.

Fire over the mountain also suggests a volcano forcing nearby people to flee. Compulsory travel is another meaning of this hexagram. Journeys are inevitable for refugees, fugitives, nomads, immigrants, seekers of a new life, and the kind of footloose wanderers who dislike staying too long in one place.

A traveler or a stranger is regarded with suspicion. I Ching commentators seem to suggest that the wanderer will bring calamity on folk of more settled habits, even though he may attain distinction among them. Homelessness is not an enviable status.

Centaurs symbolized nomadism through Eurasia in ancient times, from the Hindu *kinnaras* or horse-men to the horse cults of Iron Age Britain. Nomadic tribes from Central Asia rode as if fused with their ponies, giving all mythologies an image of the restless, savage, peripatetic wanderer, wise in magic and formidable in battle.

Among historical figures from the knight-errant or gypsy to the cowboy, man and horse together represented constant roving over the face of the earth, as of those displaced from ownership of land, home, or roots. Yet, paradoxically, the words for a man on horseback meant a nobleman (landowner): *equitis, chevalier, caballero, Ritter*, cavalier, knight. Even the Greeks regarded centaurs as "nature's noblemen" and made them great teachers of magic and philosophy.

Thunder
over
Mountain

52. *Smallness,*
Details (Hsiao Kuo)

When there is thunder over the mountain, those who stand tall and proud like big trees are at risk. Those who hide away below, like small plants and animals, avoid risk. This hexagram counsels concentration on small things, attention to detail, conscientiousness, and modesty. Not even the tiniest error should go unnoticed or uncorrected. In the end, the humble may be more favored by fortune (or by the stormy elements) than great trees that aspire toward the heavens.

Some commentators saw in the appearance of this hexagram the image of a small bird flying: the body formed by the two central lines, the wings by the upper and lower broken lines. They advised against trying to mount too high into the stormy winds. Small birds can be dashed against the mountain. They said that it is better to descend than to ascend, because descent is natural to small creatures.

After establishment of a new, aggressive religion among the great ones (that is, any priestly/military ruling caste), the world's "little people" or common folk often continued to worship their ancestral deities in secret. Sometimes the latter took the forms of Little People good at hiding themselves: elves, fairies, hobgoblins, gnomes, and other so-called demons. Europe's pagans took their ancient religion underground in this way, perpetuating the "fairy faith" even up to the time of the Renaissance and beyond.

Fairies were sometimes described as ordinary women, the matriarchs of ancient tribes. Or, they were matriarchal deities who gave the gifts of poesy and prophecy in opposition to the official church. Or, they were little sprites who helped the poor get along in a hard, cruel world. Fairies were supposed to be perceptible to the eyes of naive sensitives, such as small children and animals, but not to those of the proud rulers. Therefore, a hidden winged fairy might be seen by a knight's horse but not by the knight himself, as he rides along bearing the arrogant symbol of the thunderbolt toward his future battles.

Breath
over
Mountain

53. *Development, Progress, Partnership* (Chien)

This hexagram appears at the same place in both King Wen and Fu Hsi systems, which may have influenced the sages' interpretation: a union between two individuals, like a marriage. Increasing fortune and felicity were predicted as a result of a well-considered partnership.

The King Wen arrangement paired this hexagram with its mirror image, Fu Hsi's number 13, the Marriageable Maiden, with the implication that marriage would mean development of a husband at the wife's expense. Therefore the hexagram of partnership could signify a change from earlier views of personal progress through relationship, to the Confucian idea of female subordination. If women could be made to concentrate on small matters alone, their interests could be narrowed and belittled.

The mountain breeze is said to nurture plants with gentle rains, while the trees grow slowly, clamping the soil in place with their roots. This is likened to the gradual development of a relationship, settling the nature of the interaction one way or another. Only slow development can reveal which partner will be the more dependent of the two, which the more aggressive, which the more committed. Once the patterns are established and practiced, they become habitual, keeping the same basic form as the relationship continues to develop. Therefore, women desiring their own personal progress toward better or higher things should be careful not to throw all their energy into helping a partner get on but reserve something for themselves. Close partnership can be either progressive or constraining, according to the way it is handled by the two parties.

Water
over
Mountain

54. Trouble, Obstacles, Difficulty (Chien)

Though this hexagram has the same Chinese title as the preceding one, its intonation and meanings are different. Instead of gentle breezes over the mountain, indicating growth and development, this image suggests abundant rainfall leading to flash floods, cataracts, mud slides, or avalanches blocking the road ahead: unforeseen difficulties or dangers. What seems normally benevolent, even essential, like water, may become inimical. There may be overwhelming violence like that of a bursting dam. Water on a plain flows gently, but water comes down a mountain with force.

Interpreters of this hexagram counsel patience and care to eliminate internal causes of trouble, which may lie within one's own power to control. An ineffectual attempt at control only makes matters worse. Some said the help of a more powerful person or spirit is essential in times of trouble.

Oriental sages often used water to symbolize the feminine principle of love generated and sustained by shared sensual pleasures. Yet the fundamentally ascetic patriarchal spirit was frequently incapable of appropriate response to this idea. Ascetics tended to belittle, then diabolize, then abjectly fear the sensualities that most women associated with feelings of connectedness. Fears were embodied in the night-demonesses that were supposed to suck out men's souls in nocturnal carnality.

Westerners called the demonesses succubae, empusae, lamias, or daughters of Lilith and believed in their real existence. Like the normally containable water element raging out of control, inimical to men's interests, female spirits of irresistible lustiness were always viewed as trouble indeed.

Mountain
over
Mountain

55. *Stillness, Mountain, Solitude, Meditation* (Ken)

Double mountain symbols mean immobility, like that of a sage deep in a meditative trance on a holy mountain. There is a need for cessation of activity, contemplative quietness, and withdrawal from the busy world for self-refreshment and self-renewal.

As mountain peaks used to represent the "many-breasted" or "deep-breasted" Great Mother, source of the streams and rivers vital to the sustenance of her lowland children, so it was accepted that spiritual sustenance came from the same heights.

Even the most heroic gods or deified kings retired to their quiet paradise on the Goddess's lap, which was often called a holy mountain, to be revitalized by her nurturing embrace. Some myths mention rebirth from the womb of the Mountain Mother after a period of infantile or embryonic dependency. The hexagram of the Mountain is accordingly labeled the mysterious place where all things begin and end, where birth and death merge.

Stillness like the sage's period of contemplation—symbolic death— may be necessary after difficulties and troubles, to regroup one's inner forces for a rebirth of the personality. It may be especially necessary for women, many of whom yearn for some refreshment of solitude, in the midst of lives of perpetual relatedness and responsibility. Patriarchal males knew that creativity may be best served by solitary introspection and so tended to insist that women should be kept too busy with mundane tasks to have time or space to be alone and think their own (perhaps seditious) thoughts. Nonetheless, the need for creative stillness exists in both sexes. Women of accomplishment have been known to remark that their primary need was for "a room of one's own," or a space of solitude.

Earth
over
Mountain

56. *Modesty,*
Moderation (Ch'ien)

Stillness and immobility teach the sage to be modest, as is fitting for one truly enlightened. Having buried itself away from the sun's glare, the mole sees no difference between the darkness a few inches underground and the darkness thousands of feet deep beneath the roots of a mountain. So the modest person, as retiring as a mole, ignores the apparent highs and lows on the surface of things and seeks the deeper levels.

As Earth levels the high mountain, so those who are highly placed must be brought low, and the humble will prosper in the end. Those in high position win the love of others only by becoming modest. The wise have always counseled moderation and equilibrium, avoidance of ostentation, and a becoming lack of hubris, regarding humility as a proper path to ultimate success.

Under a patriarchal regime, women were forced to give appearances of modesty and humility, and to hide their true thoughts. However, women together might seek deeper levels in secret, avoiding the sun's glare, teaching each other under the cool light of their ancient deity, the moon. It was even said that God wouldn't listen to the prayers of women; they should address themselves to the moon instead. Such were the roots of what men called witchcraft, in periods of history when woman's nature was to men an unknown and forbidden territory hidden under the surface.

The ever-popular revolutionary type of prophecy, saying the mighty will fall and the last shall be first, echoed in the ears of the mighty and made them nervous. It was especially true in intensely patriarchal ages, when many suffered oppression and rulers had ample cause to feel guilty. A possible revolution of women against male authority was feared perhaps most of all, since universal feminine denial of men's wants could disrupt their world very thoroughly indeed.

≡ ≡

11

The Eighth Octave (K'un)

Having learned the lesson of due modesty counseled by the preceding hexagram, one may approach the final division of the I Ching, the realm of Mother Earth embodied in the eighth octave. Just as the figure of the Naked Goddess called The World (the soul of Earth) completed the progressive revelations of the Tarot trumps, so the essence of the world mother seemed to crown the progressive revelations of the I Ching. Many religious and philosophical systems, traceable to prepatriarchal times, attribute all forms of divination and prophecy to this world mother in the beginning. She alone knew all the secrets of fate and natural law.

Perhaps the spectrum of the I Ching between Air and Earth meant to evoke the old myth in which all things were contained between Mother Earth and Father Heaven. At first, the two lay too close together to allow their offspring any light or air—the usual image of primordial darkness. This trouble was caused by the father's hostility toward the children, one of whom (the usual Oedipal hero) finally ended the darkness by forcing the parental deities apart.

In Greece the same mythic theme depicted the father's castration by the son, at the behest of Mother Earth herself, who wanted her chidren to live. Even the patriarchal Olympian gods took their sacred oaths upon her name, because she was the mother of them all and the arbiter of their fortunes. In Scandinavia she was called Erda, Urd, or Wurd (Weird), the Word of Destiny, eldest of the Norns, ruler of all the gods. Until patriarchal priesthoods began to restrict her realm to "mindless matter" and to

103

arrogate the qualities of spirit and intelligence to male deities, Mother Earth used to be the fountainhead of creation, ideation, and inspiration.

In the old world of mother-religion, matter and spirit were virtually indistinguishable. Mother-blood was the "life" or soul of all beings, as well as the primal substance of all bodies. Mother Earth formed from her own blood, and then gave birth to, the sky, the mountains, the sea, the elemental spirits, the giants in the underworld, and all the father gods as well. Earth is still called "mother" almost everywhere in the world. Nazi Germany with its cult of the warrior and its severe militarism was the only recently well-known "fatherland" as opposed to a "motherland." Even when the patriarchal Bible speaks of "the land of our fathers," the land itself is female.

Air
over
Earth

57. *Stagnation, Standstill* (P'i)

This hexagram is usually interpreted to mean that the forces of nature (yang and yin) are immobilized in their separate spheres, so there is no intermingling or interchange to spark creative action. When male and female are closed off from one another, they have no power to revitalize.

Air over Earth may also refer to the original condition of stagnation when Father Heaven lay too closely on his consort Mother Earth and allowed no breath or movement to penetrate to their offspring. Their environment became stagnant.

Apathy is the keynote of a time governed by this symbol. Attempts to influence others may meet with insurmountable difficulty. A motionless period is characterized by rejection, mistrust, and leaders out of touch with followers. An inertia so profound may threaten the basic processes of life. The standstill must be broken by some form of positive action.

Classic symbol of the need to mingle male and female principles, for the sake of renewed creativity, was the satyr god, representing various human/animal consorts of the Goddess. Destruction of the natural world at the hands of violent men would have been especially distressing to him. He was always a lover of the wild woodland (represented by Artemis or Diana), the fertile earth (Demeter or Ceres), and the pure waters (Aphrodite, Venus). Disdaining such manly pursuits as war, he simply made music at the inspiration of his Muse. It was thought that after the final war at the end of the world, he would be left alone, sadly playing the earth's funeral dirge in the darkness of ultimate night, waiting for the creation of a new earth.

Sea
over
Earth

58. *Assembling,*
Gathering (Ts'ui)

Sea and Earth, the two great womb symbols, combine to suggest a mighty host and a great public ceremony, anciently represented by the offering of many sacrifices and a "sea" of faces gathered to witness the event. A group is assembled to share a common goal. To offset the stagnation of the previous hexagram, there comes a new enthusiasm to arise together with one's fellows from a position of immobility or helplessness. Forces join together to build up strength.

Sea over Earth recalls the very ancient Oriental myth of creation by raising the earth from the depths of the sea, so that some of the land could dry out and support air-breathing creatures, which then multiplied into great hosts. Many must come together in harmony for achievement of a goal. Bonds of mutual commitment are important in the collective effort.

Ancient paganism created sacrificial ceremonies in which the flesh of male animals became the "host" (Latin *hostia*, "victim"), assimilated to the Horned God and, consequently, to worshippers who partook of the communion feast. Under such names as the Lupercalia in Rome, the Heroantheia in Greece, or the Yom Kippur in Palestine, such ceremonies were supposed to relieve the burden of sins and purify the gathering for a new season of fertility and growth.

Christianity condemned such practices, after having copied enough of their basic rationale to serve its own purposes, and thriftily reduced the sacrificial feast to a minimally nourishing fragment of bread. Then the older ceremonies were called withcraft and/or devil worship, especially if they retained any trace of the formerly authoritative Great Goddess figure. Even though those who remembered and perpetuated the old ways became fewer, heretical gatherings never really ceased. Some said only the Goddess's motherly presence could reactivate creativity in a sterile world.

Fire over Earth

59. *Progress* (Chin)

Fire blazing over the rim of the earth—a rising sun—indicates accelerating progress, now that the assembly of many cooperating individuals has overcome inertia. A great leader or a great idea is like the en-lightening lightning bolt or the first rays of the sun, igniting a beacon for others to strive toward.

Ancient interpreters envisioned a mighty prince whose army possessed many horses, the animal symbols of swift motion. The leader's manifold blessings are said to emanate from his "grandmother," perhaps a euphemism for the Earth Goddess herself. She was usually assumed to be the source of every ruler's good fortune, just as in the guise of Fortuna Regia or Fortuna Augusta she supported the emperors of Rome.

Progress and its attendant enthusiasm feed on each other and move at an ever-faster pace, before they reach the end of their impetus and eventually burn out.

A typical hero emerges fully mature from the earth, golden and powerful like the sun. Indeed, many heroes and godlike leaders in mythology represented nothing other than the sun. Even Jesus was given the sun god's titles, Light of the World, Sun of Righteousness, Sol Invictus, Helios. The hero is armed with a fiery weapon symbolic of striking rays of light. His golden hair, like that of Apollo, signifies sun rays. However, in the earliest myths he didn't stand alone. It was his mother, the old Earth Goddess, who protected him, empowered him, and gave him rebirth each day.

Thunder
over
Earth

60. Repose, Harmony (Yu)

Calm confidence and some well-earned relaxation follow a progressive period, when optimism seems justified and workers take quiet pride in a job well done. Repose comes easily to those who feel a sense of accomplishment.

In this hexagram, thunder over the earth seems to suggest not a condition of storm but the gentle muttering of retreating thunder when the ground has been well watered and can rest in the confidence of future prosperity. The sages mention music—sweet sounds to soothe the ear and the mind—rather than the immediate crashing of the nearby thunder. There is harmony, like the colors of a rainbow.

Comfortable relaxation of mind and body together accompanies harmony. Like the thunder, disturbing thoughts and anxieties retreat to a safe distance. There has been a great effort, and repose is needed.

A room full of warm, soothing colors suggests repose, while cyclic alternation of rest and activity symbolically divides the space in half with two different walls: one yellow as sunlight, with an open window, the other black as night, decorated with gold stars. A filmy curtain between the two indicates the veil of twilight and dawn. A sleeper's head lies on the night side, yet her feet point toward the active movement of the daytime.

Breath
over
Earth

61. *Contemplation*

(Kuan)

Having achieved an eminence and a period of repose, any person or group of people may have leisure to devote to contemplation and higher thoughts. The enlightened one may enter upon a period of quiet withdrawal to assess the meanings and implications of what has been attained. Real progress must include some time given to the achievement of philosophical understanding.

This hexagram denotes looking down from a high place, like the enlightened sage upon a breezy mountaintop, mingling breath with the wind. One who reaches the heights should engage in an insightful assessment of the self and the surroundings, which become one in breathing. Quiet breath taken in at a place high above the earth is like a breath of inspiration (literally, "in-breathing" the spirit). The enlightened one contemplates all things as a part of herself, like the I-dea or "Goddess Within."

A significant object of group contemplation in Oriental legend was a precious talisman of the old Goddess, guarded by holy women in a mysterious womb temple on some faraway mountain. Variously described as a heart, a ruby, a crescent moon, or a cup, this talisman was Christianized as the Holy Grail, after it had been picked up from Arabic tales by European troubadours. Its Christianization was late and shallow. Earlier stories suggest that the Grail temple housed a symbol of the female, lunar Blood of Life. Contemplation of the holy object, whatever it was, gave women of the Grail temple a more than human grace, prescience, and spiritual power.

Water ⚏
over ⚏
Earth ⚏

62. *Unity, Joining, Coordination* (Pi)

As shown by the preceding hexagram, contemplation of the human condition reveals that the only real strength of human beings lies in their cooperation with one another. Therefore, true wisdom knows that the rules for interpersonal behavior patterns are basic to all human creations.

This hexagram indicates that when separate individuals or groups join together, like small waters flowing over the earth to merge in mighty rivers, the power of all component parts is greatly increased. Social rules dating from the matriarchal age emphasized cooperation, togetherness, and peaceful, harmonious, egalitarian relationships.

Another matriarchal symbol of human unity is water in an earthen vessel: a miniature representation of the primal abyss that gave birth to all creatures and of the smooth merging of separate waters (drops) into a unified whole, sheltered and given shape within the embrace of Earth.

Unity is expressed in the joining of women, who can overlook their superficial differences of color and outlook, realizing their complete identity of basic structure. In feminist spiritual thought, there could be no polarities of we/they, black/white, saved/damned, or even male/female, but rather a human unity sharing common experiences of birth, life, and death under the inexorably cyclic Mother Moon. White dog and black dog represent day and night cycles, joining together in time's progress. According to the religions of the Goddess, dogs guarded the transitional gates of death. On the other side of the gates lay a literal union with the Mother that led to rebirth. In this way her time cycles brought about unity of all things, for they were all together made of the same matter.

Mountain
over
Earth

63. Splitting, Peeling Off, Deterioration (Po)

As each movement in human life begets an equal and opposite movement, so the hexagram of unity is followed by one representing separation. Human alliances are limited. Families may be separated by circumstance, death, or the failure of love. Commercial organizations are not stable forever. Special-interest groups form and re-form. Friendships may perish. Even the component atoms and molecules of the individual body must eventually split apart and become something else.

Mountain over the earth shows that heavy support is needed for a heavy weight, but the support may fail just as an avalanche may peel off the mountain. The stairway to heaven is neither easy nor permanently stable.

Therefore, this hexagram teaches one of the sages' most valuable lessons: Nothing is forever. All human matters have their temporal limits. Not even the seemingly eternal mountains, not even the very earth itself, can exist in what might be called eternity. To speak of eternity is foolish, since the human mind can have no real comprehension of any such idea.

The Crone or Destroyer aspect of the Goddess used to formalize recognition of the natural forces of deterioration and decay, without which there could be no living existence at all. She gave men or gods the magic apples of immortality from the Tree of Life in her western garden of paradise (Jambu Island, Avalon, Elysium, the Hesperides, the Fortunate Isles, Fairyland). She also trapped their souls in her magic mirror, representing the Deep, which led to superstitions about mirrors, ghosts, and bodies of water. Like Morgan Le Fay of the Arthurian legends, the Crone-Goddess controlled the scythe of time that cut every life sooner or later and determined each season of reaping. Through her, everything returned to the earth just as the Fu Hsi system came at last to the quintessential Earth symbol.

Earth
over
Earth

64. *Nature, Earth, Creation* (K'un)

The series that began with all lines rigidly solid ends here with a double Earth sign, all lines open. Earth above and below speaks of the body born of earth, walking the earth, and eventually lying under the earth: the Oriental version of "dust to dust." The Fu Hsi arrangement ends with all bonds of matter sundered, all rigidities of structure let go, and all life's vicissitudes ended by a return to the fertile depths of the tomb-womb. This is never a conscious goal, yet it is the only real goal of all life's forms, which return to the earth whether they will or not.

Oriental sages said long before Confucius, Buddha, or Mohammed that the Earth Mother was their beginning and their end. She represented both spirit and nature, before patriarchs separated spirit from nature, calling the former "male" and thus "higher." Mother Nature embodied in the all-devouring Earth had her fearsome side. I Ching commentators likened her sign to a dark, enchanted valley, a great vessel, a repository of seed, and other female-symbolic forms. Sometimes, K'un was represented by a mare, like the many equine disguises of the Mother in Western traditions: Leukippe the "White Mare" of Crete, Epona the Mare-goddess of Iron Age Britain, or mare-headed Black Demeter as the avenging Night-Mare in her sacred cave at Mavrospelya.

The I Ching also emphasized the creative, nurturing power of the earth, signified by the color yellow—gold, ripe fruit, honey, the yolk of the cosmic egg—as contrasted with the black of the underworld. Yet the yellow and the black must alternate like tiger stripes, like day and night. Nu-Kua or Kuan-Yin, China's Earth-Mother-Nature-Creatress, spoke the last word on the I Ching as on every living form, which would return always to her eternal flux. A yellow diamond was one of her most common symbols, combining the ideas of earth's primary treasures, gold and diamonds, in a figure recognized nearly everywhere as the shape of a yoni—though sometimes, men's iconography tipped it over into the yellow "Earth Square."

Ancient Europe personified the all-devouring Earth Mother as Hel, or Holde, or Holle, or Halja, who dwelt in the underworld with her mighty serpent, her first consort. She presided over the earth cauldron where all forms of life were recombined and recycled. Some, who were lucky enough to wear the helmet called Helkappe, would be able to visit her and yet return alive to the upper world.

She favored the Helleder, men who had died heroically. Though her name gave us "hell," her underground realm was not the place of punishment it later became. Like the earth itself, Hel simply received the dead and cared for them. Her worshipers claimed to be revitalized in her underworld cauldron, because they returned to the source of creative energy and received new forms. This idea exerted some influence on the Christian doctrine of purgatory, which was not clearly distinguished from hell (or Hel) until the Middle Ages were well advanced.

Like the Earth principle underlying the earth reality, Hel was called the source of all children who are born and at the same time the receptacle of all the souls of the dead. In other words, she was what all forms of the Great Mother had been from the beginning.

Bibliography

Blofeld, John, trans. *I Ching, the Book of Change*. New York: Dutton, 1968.

Legge, James, trans. *I Ching, Book of Changes*. New York: University Books, 1964.

Miller, Terry. *Images of Change: Paintings on the I Ching*. New York: Dutton, 1976.

Wilhelm, Richard, trans. *The Secret of the Golden Flower: A Chinese Book of Life*. New York: Harcourt, Brace & World, 1962.

Wing, R. L. *The Illustrated I Ching*. New York: Doubleday, 1982.